How to
Catch
Bottomfish

How to Catch Bottomfish

Charlie White

Heritage
House

National Library of Canada Cataloguing in Publication Data

White, Charles, 1925–
　　How to catch bottomfish / Charlie White.

　　ISBN 1-894384-60-1

　　1. Bottom fishing. I. Title.

SH455.6.W55 2003　　　799.1'22　　　C2003-910183-5

First edition 1974　　　Reprinted 1976, 1979, 1986, 1988
Second edition 1992, first Heritage edition 2003.

　　Heritage House acknowledges the financial support for our publishing program from the Government of Canada through the Book Publishing Industry Development Program (BPIDP), Canada Council for the Arts, and the British Columbia Arts Council.

Cover design and layout: Darlene Nickull
Cover photos: Robert H. Jones
Illustrations: Nelson Dewey

HERITAGE HOUSE PUBLISHING COMPANY LTD.
#108 – 17665 66A Ave., Surrey, BC V3S 2A7

Printed in Canada

CONTENTS

AN IMPORTANT REMINDER!

Do not go fishing in B.C. without first studying the current *B.C. Tidal Waters Sport Fishing Guide*, published annually by Fisheries and Oceans Canada. It is available free of charge at sporting-goods stores, marinas, and similar outlets. The guide contains all regulations governing sport fishing for salmon, halibut, rockfish, crabs, oysters, and other species. Check carefully the sections on spot closures, which were introduced as a conservation measure to protect not only salmon, but also crabs, lingcod, and many other species.

On page 126, you'll find a list of websites that contain up-to-date regulations.

INTRODUCTION

When we prepared our first booklet on bottomfish, we had no idea how many people would be interested enough to pay for the information. As this seventh printing goes to press in greatly expanded form (more than four times as much material as in the original edition), we are grateful for the continuing response.

With the increasing pressure of our daily lives, a relaxing day on the water has strong appeal. We are very fortunate in the Pacific Northwest to have lots of open air and unpolluted water to enjoy.

In this book, we deal with the best known of the edible saltwater fishes of the North Pacific coast (excluding salmon, which is covered in detail in *How to Catch Salmon: Basic Fundamentals*: this popular book is a continuing bestseller, with sales now over 140,000). Most of these species dwell on or near the bottom (within five or six feet of the sand, mud, rock, or gravel), except for perch, which is a mid-water fish.

These fish are often scorned by sport fishermen who spend all of their time chasing (often futilely!) the more glamorous and spectacular fighting salmon. There is no doubt that catching a salmon is one of the peak experiences in the fishing world and makes the best material for "fish stories" back home or with the boys in the office. However, there are

many, many times when the salmon just are not in your area or they stubbornly refuse to bite. (At the best of times, the salmon will only feed for a short time each day.) At these times, the angler can either patiently fish for salmon, with only a small chance of success, or try for bottomfish.

These bottom dwellers can provide lots of excitement and a very tasty meal to boot. Most species are delicious for eating—many people prefer them to salmon. To the great mass

" ...A TASTY MEAL TO BOOT. "

of freshwater fishermen in North America, the bottomfish of the North Pacific ocean are bigger, harder fighting, and better eating than anything they have ever caught in fresh water!

Bottomfishing doesn't require expensive equipment. A simple single-action reel, almost any kind of rod, some hooks, and bait are all that is needed, especially for beginners.

You don't even need a boat for many types of bottomfish. Many can be taken right from the shore, especially on rocky drop-offs. Piers and wharves are also excellent locations for bottomfishing.

However, a small dinghy or aluminum boat with outboard will allow you to cover a lot of productive water. Some types of fish are found mostly in deep water and on sandy bottoms away from shorelines. You could build a raft and play Tom Sawyer to get to these fish, but rafts are difficult to handle and can be very dangerous if the wind comes up.

Fishing from a boat has the added advantage of allowing you to drift effortlessly with wind or tide over a wide area; the shorebound angler can work only a very limited area of shoreline where conditions are suitable.

The late Sidney Girling wrote a comprehensive section of this book, outlining in meticulous detail the methods he used for catching bottomfish from a rowing dinghy. His detailed records of his many trips list impressive and consistent catches of bottomfish.

Mr. Girling specialized in fishing the rocky reefs, and the majority of his catch has been rockfish and lingcod. However, he has caught many other types of bottomfish. He even had an hour-long battle with a huge halibut. A version of the octopus-type lure he developed and describes in this book is now available at sporting-goods stores.

Chapter 1
EQUIPMENT

You can catch bottomfish quite successfully using a handline, but an inexpensive rod and reel makes it easier and more fun. If a fish begins swimming toward the boat, it is awkward to keep proper tension with a handline. A rod helps take the shock out of sudden lunges by the fish. It also gives you more control in guiding the line around and under the boat as the fish dashes frantically for freedom.

Choosing a Rod

When bottom jigging for rockfish, lingcod, red snapper, and other heavy fish, a relatively short rod of medium stiffness is most appropriate. A one-piece fibreglass rod of about five and a half to six and a half feet is quite inexpensive and works well.

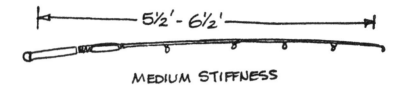

MEDIUM STIFFNESS

Somewhat longer rods, up to seven and a half feet, are also good, but these are usually two-piece and more expensive. If they are stiff enough, longer rods give more leverage in handling a fish. You can exert a strong, steady force to lift big ones off the bottom. A longer flexible rod gives more shock-absorbing action against a fish's hook-tearing jerks. However, this shock-absorbing action can absorb your leverage when you're trying to hold a fish off the bottom.

On the other hand, the shorter rod is much more convenient to handle in a small boat. While rigging tackle or changing baits, you want to be able to rest the rod in the boat. If most of it is hanging over the side, it is difficult to reach the tip to grasp the line.

There is also the danger of knocking the whole outfit into the sea. I had this experience with one of my sons, then aged nine. He had just landed a lovely big sole, which we were admiring as it flopped in the bottom of our twelve-foot boat.

I dispatched it with a sharp blow to its head and bent down to dislodge the hooks. I heard a splash and felt a tug on the line leading from the hook. Looking up, I saw the line leading over the side and straight down into 100 feet of water.

The rod and reel had been resting across the gunwales, and the boat had tipped somewhat as I bent over the fish. The whole outfit slid into the sea before I realized what was happening. A shorter rod would have been inside the boat.

Summing up on rods, I feel a short, one-piece fibreglass model is the best bet for most bottomfish. (A lighter, flexible rod is more suitable for jigging for sole and other small flatfish.) These will be inexpensive and of satisfactory quality if purchased from a reputable dealer. Even the cheapest fibreglass rods will stand a lot of abuse.

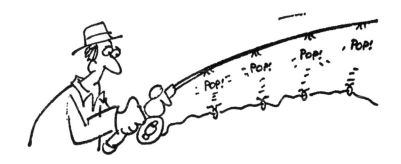

The major differences between a quality rod and a cheap one are in the line guides, their wrappings, and in the reel seating arrangement. Cheap line guides will be made of light or brittle metal, which tends to bend or break more easily with rough treatment. The wrappings that hold the line guides on the low-priced rods tend to come unravelled.

Reel seats made of light metal can twist under pressure. Movable reel seats are supposed to have the advantage of adjusting the reel to the most convenient distance from the butt. The problem with them is that they keep on adjusting while in use. The reels often twist sideways (out of line with the rod), rotate around the rod, or fall off altogether.

If you plan to fish for salmon as well as bottomfish, I would suggest a longer rod. It should be at least seven feet long, but preferably eight or eight and a half. It should have a sturdy butt and a soft, flexible tip. The sturdy butt section will give you the power to control a good-sized fish and the flexible tip is advantageous as the shock absorber.

For heavy fish, you might want to employ Mr. Girling's technique of dropping the line down from a guide nearer the butt to give the effect of a short rod. (His technique is discussed later in this book.)

Choosing a Reel

My favourite reel is the centre-pin, single-action type. It consists of a spool of line with handles, which revolves around a centre pin mounted in a housing with an extending bracket for attaching to a rod. There is usually a ratchet device to warn of a strike and provide that delightful zinging sound when the fish runs and pulls out line.

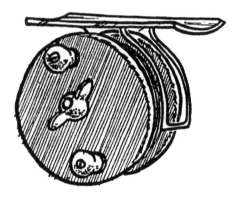

These reels are usually inexpensive and their simplicity makes them practically maintenance-free. A little grease on the centre pin and on the ratchet pivot points is all that is needed to keep them trouble-free for years.

Some people feel that the star-drag reels, which slip when the fish pulls, have some advantages. However, I don't like them at all. They eliminate the "feel" of the fish, which you get by manually controlling the single-action reel with the palm of your hand.

Single-action reels have been nicknamed "knuckle-dusters" because they can bark the skin on your knuckles if you grab for the whirling handles. However, it is very easy to learn the proper technique, and it's a thrilling sensation to feel the force of the running fish as the reel spins against your hand-braking action. (My three young sons have handled fish up to 50 pounds using these reels.)

Star-drag reels do have a multiplying gear action that allows fast retrieval if a fish heads for the boat, but I have always been able to take up this slack successfully with my knuckle-dusters.

Star-drag reels allow you to just keep winding the handle while the action of the star drag (a slipping clutch arrangement) gives line to the fish when it pulls. You can actually reel in while the fish runs out. While this automatic feature has some advantage for those who haven't learned the simple technique of controlling a single-action reel, it can cause problems when landing a fish.

If a heavy fish keeps pulling when close to the boat, you may be tempted to tighten down on the drag. This allows you to pull harder without reel slip and haul the fish to the net or gaff. The fish, seeing the landing device, often makes one last dash for freedom and breaks the leader or tears out the hooks.

Spinning reels are the obvious choice for the caster. They allow long, tangle-free casts and are relatively easy to learn to use. I would suggest a saltwater model, which is made to stand up in corrosive conditions. Saltwater reels are also designed for heavier lines.

Spinning reels call for a longer, more flexible rod to give that snap to the lure when casting. Any knowledgeable fishing-tackle salesperson should be able to recommend a good combination of rod and spinning reel for your particular purpose.

I often use a spinning outfit when jigging for sole. It is a lightweight rod and small reel more suited to trout fishing, but it works well on the smaller flatfish. While I don't cast with it, the spinning reel allows the line to drop freely and quickly. The light, flexible rod shows nibbles on its sensitive tip and makes it easier to play the soft-mouthed sole.

For surfcasting, a long, heavy, flexible rod and heavy-duty casting or spinning reel is needed. The side-cast reels, which rotate 90 degrees on the reel seat, are becoming very popular. Their large spools allow the use of heavier lines and have the advantages of a spinning reel cast. Before winding in, the reel rotates to a position parallel with the rod. Now you can wind in with the positive control of a single-action reel.

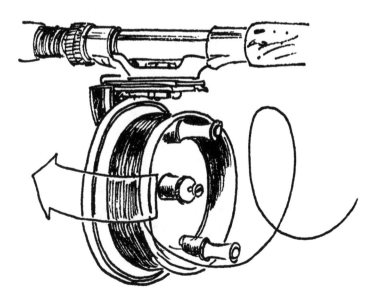

Line

While some braided Dacron or braided nylon lines are used for bottomfishing, the most popular is nylon monofilament. This type of line is inexpensive and is practically invisible underwater. Its smooth surface allows for easy casting and retrieving.

Nylon is an elastic material and will stretch under tension. This is both an advantage and a disadvantage, depending on how you use it. A stretching line is an advantage in absorbing shocks from a surging, jerking fish that might otherwise tear loose.

On the other hand, an elastic line can be a drawback when you're trying to pull a heavy fish off the bottom before it can bury itself under a rock or wrap the line around a boulder. Nylon's stretch can also damage a reel when wound on too tightly.

If you reel in a large fish under a lot of pressure, the line will still be stretched as it wraps onto the drum of the reel. The same thing happens when you wind in a heavy load of kelp, other seaweed, or a snagged piece of wood or other debris.

After you have many turns of this tightly stretched line on the reel, a tremendous crushing force is exerted against the core and sides of the reel drum. Plastic reels will often split wide open under this pressure. (The pressure often doesn't crack the reel immediately, but many anglers have been startled to find a broken reel the next day.)

Better-quality reels, of metal or fibreglass reinforced plastic, will stand a great deal of line pressure, but even these will distort or twist slightly.

If you plan to do heavy fishing, it is a good idea to put several layers of a softer, braided line on the reel's core before adding the nylon. This will absorb a lot of the pressure.

However, the only certain method of preventing reel damage is to strip the line off again as soon as possible after winding it on under pressure. Then you can reel it in again without undue strain on it.

Some of the newer Dacron braided lines will not stretch, but their opaque appearance is a drawback. Their rougher surface, caused by the braiding, increases line drag in the water.

The strength of line to use depends on the size of the fish you are likely to catch. Different line is required for casting and trolling than for jigging and stillfishing.

When casting or trolling, heavier lines have some disadvantages. Heavy casting lines, especially for spinning, tend to be too stiff for smooth pulling off the end of the spinning reel spool.

A limp nylon line is best for spinning. These also tend to be quite soft, which means they will nick and fray easily. Soft nylons also tend to crush in knots, weakening the knot considerably. New-technology nylons, however, combine a tough skin with limpness and more strength with the same thickness.

When trolling, heavy lines increase friction drag and hold the lure nearer the surface. Since bottomfish are, by definition, on the bottom, this is undesirable. Trolling at a slower speed will overcome this problem to some extent.

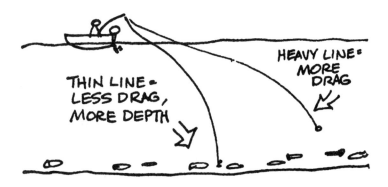

Heavy lines are not a problem when jigging or stillfishing. There is not much line drag, unless you're fishing in a strong tidal current. Line is simply stripped off the reel until it hits bottom, so there are no casting problems.

Jigging for rockfish and lingcod is almost always over a rocky, often jagged bottom, and it is very easy to snag the bottom. Heavy line is a real advantage when pulling loose from these hang-ups. You should use lighter leaders, especially for lingcod, which seem to be fussy about striking when bulky lines are coming out of the bait.

Summing up on line strength, I would suggest the following nylon lines for the various types of bottomfishing:

Spincasting: 10- to 20-pound-test

Trolling: 20- to 25-pound-test

Jigging: 20- to 40-pound-test

Lighter lines for jigging are good, but not necessary. I use my twenty-pound-test salmon line for jigging because it is easy and convenient to use the same equipment. I just snap off my salmon lures and rig up for bottomfish.

This is much easier than carrying an extra rod and reel with heavier line. I probably lose a bit more gear by breaking lines when they get snagged on the bottom, but it is not a significant amount. However, I don't think I have lost any fish by using twenty-pound-test. (Many tyee salmon anglers land 50-pound salmon on twenty-pound-test. Two of my teenaged sons have landed salmon weighing over 53 pounds on single-action reels and twenty-pound line).

You should put at least 600 feet of line (two spools of 100 yards) on your reels if you plan to fish for large bottomfish. A big lingcod in a heavy tide can run out a lot of line. When trolling, you can also strip out several hundred feet on a bottom hang-up before you get the boat turned around.

Having extra line also allows you to follow a practice common among good fishermen everywhere. Before each outing, check the last ten feet of line for frays and nicks. Break off this portion and tie up your terminal gear to a fresh, unfrayed end.

The end of the line also deteriorates right on the reel from exposure to sunlight. Many anglers break off six to ten feet of line every few trips, even if there is no sign of wear. When a line becomes opaque and dull instead of shiny and translucent, it is time to break off this portion.

Once a year, the entire line should be removed from the reel and reversed. This will put the fresh, unused line from the core of the reel out on the working end. The end used during the previous season will then be on the inside and will seldom if ever come off the reel.

Weights

The proper weight to use for bottomfishing depends on the fishing situation. No weight at all is the most effective rig for catching big perch under a dock or pier. Fishing in a heavy tide may require six to eight ounces when jigging and a pound or more when trolling

The purpose of the weight is to get the line and lure down to the bottom where, hopefully, a hungry bottomfish is waiting. The size of weight required depends almost entirely on the forces retarding the line and lure from sinking.

If you drop a weight with no line connected to it, it plummets almost straight down. When you introduce the lure and line, they create friction drag, which slows down the speed of descent. Add a tidal current moving sideways to the direction of descent, and the situation is further complicated.

The tidal current pulls the line out horizontally proportional to the force of the current. Thicker line and light, bulky lures also increase drag. Fishing depth also affects friction drag, since more line in the water means more friction surface.

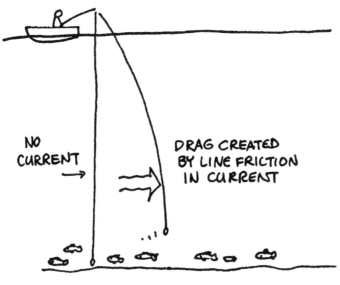

NO CURRENT

DRAG CREATED BY LINE FRICTION IN CURRENT

Generally speaking, three or four ounces is sufficient for jigging or driftfishing. In this type of fishing, the boat is moving in the same direction as the line and weight, so there is little if any line friction for the weight to overcome. If wind is blowing the boat to create a side drag on the line, add an extra ounce or two of weight until the line goes down at a reasonable angle. Line angle should usually not exceed 45 degrees from vertical.

Spherical or teardrop-shaped weights are most efficient for jigging. Crescent-shaped mooching sinkers work well, especially when drifting in a gentle current. Heavy currents may require a heavier round weight.

For trolling, many shapes of weights are available. Slip sinkers, which can be set on the line away from the lure and trip on a strike, are recommended. If the sinker is too near the lure (and moving through the water), it might distract the fish. The sinker will also catch weed on the line and keep it away from the lure.

Surfcasting requires a pyramid weight that will hold in the sand against the pull of the waves and currents.

Hooks

Buy good, strong hooks of the proper size for the variety of fish you are seeking. Many makers, particularly English manufacturers, produce different grades of hooks. They will be labelled with such phrases as "Extra Strong," "Double Extra Strong," and even "Triple Extra Strong."

Stainless-steel hooks are excellent and will last indefinitely. If they are legal in your area, I recommend using them.

Common sense is the best guide in choosing hook size. The basic rule is small hooks for small fish and larger hooks for large fish. Perch and sole require small hooks for their tiny mouths. Lingcod, rockfish, and halibut can swallow as big a hook as you can buy. Large hooks are also necessary when using live bait, so the hook can hold the bait and still protrude enough to hook the fish.

I will suggest specific hook sizes when discussing each type of bottomfish.

One last comment on hooks: Keep them sharp! A darting fish will snatch a bait and whisk away in a flash. Often it just brushes against the hook, or the hook touches a hard bony part of the fish's mouth.

A sharp hook will catch and dig in, while a dull hook will merely slide off and you will have missed your fish.

Salmon fishermen say that hooks should be "sticky-sharp." This means that the points are so sharp, they "stick" to any surface they touch. A good test is to put the point of the hook gently on your fingernail. If it sticks, your hook is sharp enough.

Sharpen your hooks before baiting them when you start out on every fishing expedition. Carry a small sharpening stone or triangular file in your tackle box for this purpose.

Many anglers don't bother with hand filing, as there are now battery-operated hook sharpeners on the market that will produce a sticky-sharp hook in seconds. Among them is one I developed, available at stores or from me for $19.95 plus tax and $4 handling at 11046 Chalet Rd., Sidney, BC, V8L 5M2.

Don't try to shine up rusty hooks. Hooks are the least expensive part of your gear. Throw them away and use fresh ones.

Swivels

You should use some type of swivel on any fishing line to prevent line twist between lure and rod tip. Lures and weights tend to turn and roll as they are lowered or raised. They also turn and twist when drifting in the tidal current.

When you hook a fish, it is likely to roll and turn as you reel it in. Some fish will even twist themselves right around the line.

A swivel between leader and main line will eliminate most of this ravelling by turning with the leader and terminal tackle. The size of swivel should be proportional to the line strength and size of terminal gear.

Perch fishing requires a very tiny swivel so as not to scare off the very wary fish. Fishing for rockfish, lingcod, and other large bottomfish calls for a larger, stronger swivel.

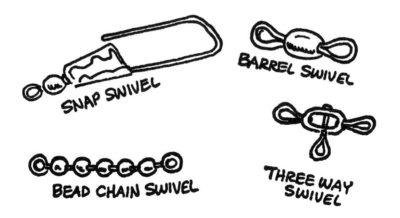

Swivels are also used as connectors for such special rigs as paternoster booms. Three-way swivels help separate gear for a number of rigs used for surfcasting, bottom jigging, or even some live-bait hookups.

Landing Nets and Gaffs

Salmon fishermen prefer nets to land their catch. A large landing net provides a wide opening into which you can guide the thrashing, jerking salmon. Using a gaff hook, it requires more skill to get the salmon on the first try. If you miss a salmon with the gaff, it often lunges free or it may even be knocked loose with the gaff.

Most bottomfish, on the other hand, tend to lie quietly on the water when brought to the surface. The rapid change in pressure from the deep water seems to take the life out of them, at least momentarily.

The air bladders of rockfish and red snapper are often so enlarged that the fish lie helplessly upside down or on their sides with bulging bellies. This makes it relatively easy to gaff them and lift them aboard.

Drive the gaff into the fish's head or gills, being careful not to gaff it in its body, as that will ruin some good meat. A gaff will tear out of flesh more easily than it will from the tougher head and gill covers. It is best to aim for the underside

of the jaw, where the gaff can enter easily and catch inside the bony edge of the jaw or under the gills. Keep the gaff very sharp or it may not penetrate properly.

Landing nets are quite satisfactory for boating bottomfish, but they can be a nuisance. Rockfish and lingcod tend to get badly tangled in the net, and it is a tedious task to untangle a flapping, twisting fish. Rockfish spines and lingcod teeth will jam in the net mesh and are difficult to remove. It is also very easy to get a nasty wound from a rockfish spine or from the sharp, pointed teeth of a ling.

A small trout net is excellent for small bottomfish without too many spines. I find it good for landing sole, sand dab, and other small flatfish. A small net might also be good for perch, but most perch fishermen I know just pull the wriggling perch straight up onto the deck with the fishing line itself.

Fish Boxes

It is desirable to have a place to store your catch on board. Fish flapping or sliding around on the deck will cause a mess, and the slime will make the surface slippery. When fishing for small sole, I often just use a big plastic bucket. However, this is not satisfactory for larger fish. There are many shapes and sizes of larger plastic containers available that make excellent fish boxes.

Baby bathtubs are perfect for all but the big lingcod. These tubs are rectangular with rounded ends, are very sturdy, and are easy to keep clean. If you want a larger box, there are some small plastic boats available in the toy section of most department stores.

You can also buy custom-made fish boxes of galvanized iron or fibreglass. Fibreglass boxes are more expensive but will last indefinitely. They also have rounded corners, which are easier to clean than the square corners of galvanized boxes.

All fish boxes should be kept covered with a burlap sack, old towel, or other absorbent cloth soaked in sea water. This will keep the fish cool and moist until you get them to shore for cleaning.

Rod Holders

When you are jigging, you will be holding your rod most of the time. However, it is convenient to have a rod holder in which to place the rod when you want to open some fresh bait, get a cup of coffee or tea, or have a bite of lunch.

Sometimes I put my rod in the holder and just pull on the line, rather than raising the rod to get the jigging action. This takes only one hand and frees the other for holding a beverage or sandwich.

When drifting for sole or rockfish, I have got many strikes when the rod was just sitting in the holder. The bait evidently triggers a strike just by bouncing near the bottom, turning in the tide.

When trolling, rod holders are almost a necessity. It is very difficult to hold a rod by hand for a long time against the drag of the tackle. Propping the rod against an oarlock or jamming it into a crevice is very unsatisfactory. Furthermore,

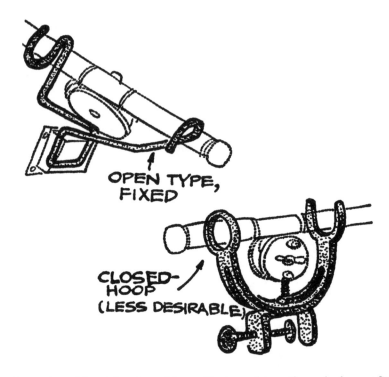

OPEN TYPE, FIXED

CLOSED-HOOP (LESS DESIRABLE)

there is a big risk of accidentally knocking the whole outfit over the side of the boat.

You don't need expensive rod holders for bottomfish. Adjustable models are useful for trolling with bucktail flies and other special salmon-fishing techniques, but have no advantage in bottomfishing.

TEMPRESS

STRIKER

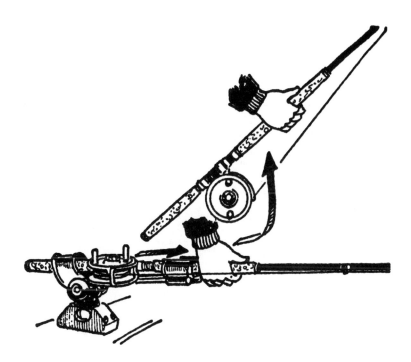

When removing a rod from the holder, always grasp it above the reel seat. Then pull the butt straight up out of the bottom of the holder. This method prevents jamming, and the rod is vertical, in proper position to strike and play the fish.

Chapter 2
BAIT

Natural Versus Artificial

Most bottomfishing is done with natural bait, but artificial lures are finding increasing acceptance. Various types of metal jigs from Scandinavian countries and feather jigs and plastic or rubber lures from Japan are used more and more frequently.

In the chapter on reef fishing, author Sidney Girling describes his success with homemade rubber octopus lures. In his opinion, properly designed artificial lures will outfish natural bait for rockfish and lingcod.

Sometimes a combination of natural and artificial bait is effective. A narrow strip of herring, pork rind, fish belly, or even cod skin can be hooked to the end of an artificial lure. This bit of natural food dangling on the end of a moving lure will often trigger a strike.

In experiments with our underwater research camera, we found that artificial-natural bait combinations were very effective for bottomfish. The productivity of jigging lures more than doubled when we added bait to the hooks.

ADD BAIT TO YOUR ARTIFICIAL LURES!

Sole, sand dabs, and sculpins were attracted to the flopping, flashing lure, but were hesitant to strike until it momentarily stopped moving. They snatched at a baited hook more readily than a bare wire one.

Jigging lures with spinner tails were extremely effective. The vibrating spinner focussed the strike on the bait and hook.

Using Scent

Our experiments also showed that adding scent to both natural and artificial lures can increase their effectiveness. Herring oil or my Formula X-10 attracted more strikes with all types of bottomfish and with salmon as well. You don't need a lot of scent. Three or four drops is usually enough, but it needs to be renewed on the lure every fifteen or twenty minutes. I usually add scent each time I bring in the lure to check it.

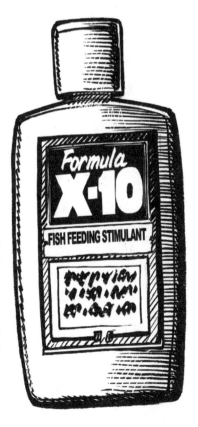

Natural Bait

There is a wide selection of natural bait available. Most can be collected right on the beach before you start fishing. Take a suitable container so the bait can be kept fresh and alive if possible.

Pile Worms and Tubeworms

These sea worms are a natural food for most bottomfish, but especially for flounder, sole, and perch. There is even a story of an old-timer who caught big chinook salmon by mooching with pile worms.

These worms resemble a centipede with many legs. They vary in colour from green to brown. They are quite firm and juicy and make an excellent bait. In fact, if I had to choose one single bait for bottomfishing, I would pick the pile worm.

Pile worms can be found between and under the clusters of barnacles and mussels on rocks, docks, and pilings. You can also find them under rocks and waterlogged pieces of driftwood. You can dig for them in the mud, gravel, or sand in the lower half of the intertidal zone. You will often find pile worms when digging for clams. (See my book *How to Catch Shellfish*.)

Other varieties of sea worms, called tubeworms, live inside a

TUBE WORM

thin, cylindrical shell. They will be found sticking out from the mussels and barnacles on floating docks and can be gathered at any stage of the tide.

Keeping pile worms alive
Pile worms keep much better in cool weather and should be kept out of the sun. If you plan to use them the same day, put them in a small box, plastic container, or bucket with some sand or fine beach gravel.

You can keep them alive for several days by cleaning off all clinging mud or sand and then wrapping them carefully in dry newspaper. Store in a cool, dry place.

Hooking pile worms
Pile worms can be threaded right up to the eye of the hook, with an inch or two left to wiggle off the point. If worms are scarce or if you are fishing for small sole, putting small chunks of worm on the tip of the hook works well.

Be careful when handling pile worms. They can bite! It is not a very painful bite, but it can be startling!

Clams

Pieces of any variety of clam make very good bait, especially for flatfish. The tougher neck sections of cockles, horse clams, and large butter clams are better than the tender parts because they stay on the hook well.

Keep clams fresh by storing them without water but covered with a moist cloth. Clams crowded in a small container of water will soon suffocate.

MOIST CLOTH

KEEP WATER (ESPECIALLY *RAIN* WATER) FROM COLLECTING IN CONTAINER.

Mussels

Mussels will be found in abundance clinging to rocks, pilings, and floating docks. Mussels can be used whole or broken into pieces for small fish. If you break up a mussel, leave bits of shell attached to the meat for a more natural-looking bait.

A whole mussel should be removed from the shell, then turned inside out and placed on the hook. This will allow its milk to flow into the surrounding water and attract the fish.

Open mussels by putting a knife blade between the tips of the shell and cutting to the hinge. They are difficult to keep on the hook, but threading the hook through a bit of shell or the toughest part of the meat will help. If you want to be fussy, you might even try holding it on by wrapping a fine thread around the shell.

Shrimp and Prawns

If you have a shrimp trap, you can save some of your catch for bottomfishing. Shrimp can also be found at low tide along the shore and against and under rocks and seaweed.

Live shrimp are very good bait, but they should be used immediately, as they do not keep well. I have kept them alive in cool weather (March) in large plastic garbage cans by changing the water every morning and evening. However, they die quickly in warm summer weather.

Shrimp and prawns can be hooked through the tail or through the back as shown.

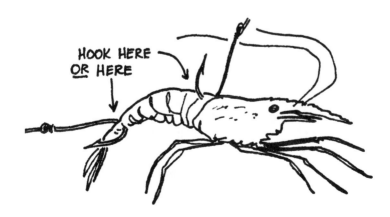

HOOK HERE
OR HERE

Shrimp tails are good bait, but it is difficult to hold the soft meat on the hook. Leave the shell on and thread carefully to avoid breaking the slight bond between meat and shell.

Ghost Shrimp

Ghost shrimp are the very soft, pale creatures found in the mud and sand when you're digging for clams. They make long oval- shaped holes as they burrow through the sand, mud, and gravel. They can be fished in a similar manner as shrimp and prawns, or they can be broken in chunks and threaded on a hook.

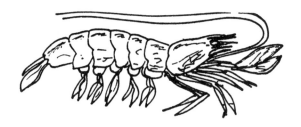

Shore Crabs

Small shore crabs are very abundant under rocks, seaweed, and almost any hiding place that is dark and moist. The soft-shelled crabs make the best bait.

All crabs grow by shedding their shells periodically and swelling up to a new, larger size. Just after they discard their old shells, they are very soft, making a tasty morsel for most bottomfish. Thread them whole on the hook.

Crabs will keep in a bucket for several days if covered with a moist cloth.

Limpets and Whelks

Limpets are easily obtained on any rocky or gravel beach. They cling to rocks or seawalls right up to the high-tide level. Gather them with a quick motion, slipping a knife between the single shell and the rock. If the limpet is alerted to your presence, it will grab the rock firmly and be much more difficult to remove.

Whelks are found near low-tide level. They can be used like limpets after you've removed them from their shells.

WHELK

Herring

Herring is the one natural bait that you can easily obtain from tackle shops or live-bait dealers. Frozen herring and herring strip can be used whole or in chunks. When I try bottomfishing after an early-morning salmon trip, my leftover herring is usually my only bait.

PLUG·CUT RIG:

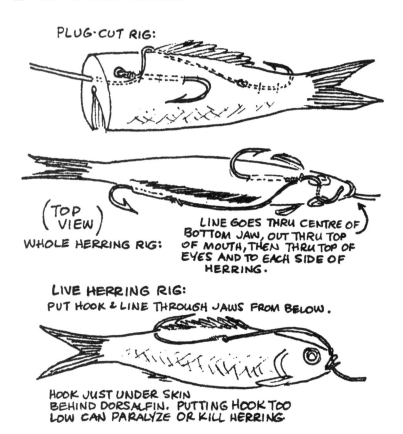

(TOP VIEW)

WHOLE HERRING RIG:

LINE GOES THRU CENTRE OF BOTTOM JAW, OUT THRU TOP OF MOUTH, THEN THRU TOP OF EYES AND TO EACH SIDE OF HERRING.

LIVE HERRING RIG:
PUT HOOK & LINE THROUGH JAWS FROM BELOW.

HOOK JUST UNDER SKIN BEHIND DORSALFIN. PUTTING HOOK TOO LOW CAN PARALYZE OR KILL HERRING.

Herring can be mooched or trolled, either whole or plug-cut, to catch rockfish and lingcod. Mooched herring is also used to catch halibut. A number of lucky anglers have landed huge halibut while mooching for salmon over sandy bottoms.

Live herring is a deadly bait for rockfish and lings. They just can't resist a live herring wriggling on a hook. Shiner perch and other small fish are also used alive in the same manner.

Herring and other baitfish can be kept alive in a large plastic garbage can if the water is changed frequently. Minnow or bait buckets that float in the water next to the boat can also be used.

Chapter 3
SOLE AND FLOUNDER

These are the real bottomfish. They lie flat on the bottom in mud or sand areas most of their lives. These flatfish are a dramatic example of how nature adapts a species for survival. Evidence shows that they are descended from a more familiar vertically oriented fish, such as a perch or freshwater sunfish. But certain fish found that by lying flat in the mud or sand, they were able to hide from enemies and lie in wait for their own food. An evolutionary process gradually changed the shape and position of certain fins and—most dramatic of all—one eye actually migrated to the other side of the head!

Even today, all flatfish begin life with eyes on both sides of the body. At a very early age, one eye moves to the other

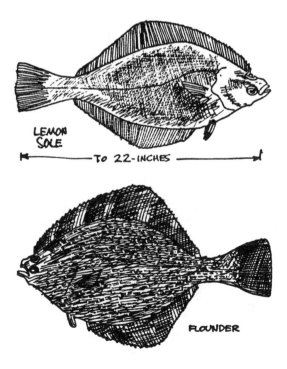

LEMON SOLE

|← ——————— TO 22-INCHES ——————— →|

FLOUNDER

side of the head so that the fish can lie flat in the sand with both eyes on the "top" side!

These fish also developed a remarkable ability to camouflage themselves. I have watched, in the Undersea Gardens, a sole swim to a sandy spot, settle to the bottom, then cover most of its body with a thin layer of sand with two quick flips of its fins!

Catching Flatfish

This habit is an important key to catching sole and flounder. Because they like to lie hidden in the sand waiting for their food, you have to get the bait in exactly the right spot in order to catch them. The best way to find a good sole bed is to ask lots of questions locally. Most good sole fishermen have definite "markers" to line up the best fishing spots.

Try to find out these precise directions rather than a general "over on that side of the bay," which will still leave you with lots of groping to do to find the spot. Knowing how

LINE UP TWO PAIRS OF PERMANENT OBJECTS.

THE CLOSER TO A 90° ANGLE BETWEEN PAIRS, THE BETTER.

90°

to use markers is important for following directions and for identifying locations you discover yourself.

New technology can replace the "gunsight marks" method. Global Positioning System (GPS) satellite technology provides a quick and easy method of keeping track of the hot spots for sole and flounder. When you start catching fish, just push the button on the GPS and you'll be able to retrieve the exact coordinates of your "fishy" spot on your next sole-fishing trip.

Some sole beds are in the middle of large bays and are difficult to locate. There is an excellent sole bed in Patricia Bay, in front of my home near Sidney. An old-time fisherman showed me how to find it using navy anchoring buoys to line up the spot.

We woke up one morning to find that the buoys had been moved to a different mooring area over a mile away. It took most of the next season to relocate this very productive spot!

Sole and flounder beds can also be located by studying marine charts. Look for a mud bottom (or sand, if need be) with a very gradual slope (a gradual slope is indicated by wide distances between depth graduation lines). They can

be found at almost any depth, from 10 to 15 feet to 150 feet or more.

Contrary to popular belief, flatfish prefer a mud bottom to sand. More tiny food organisms feed on the nutrients found in mud than in the more sterile and barren sand. These tiny organisms are eaten by larger organisms, starting the food chain that supports fish life. Fisheries department data shows that the heaviest concentrations of flatfish are found on mud bottoms.

Good sole beds can be very productive indeed!

Baiting the Hook

There are two schools of thought on this subject. Some people feel that the worm or other bait should be threaded on the hook so as to cover it completely and hide it from the fish. Others feel that the hook should be put lightly through the worm so that the bait can wriggle freely. My preference when fishing flounder and sole is to thread small chunks of worm  right onto the hook, covering the point and barb. All fish strike by instinct, not by rational thought. If they see or smell natural food, they will grab it no matter how it is hooked. Threading on small chunks saves scarce bait!

Hook size should not be too large for these small-mouthed fishes. A No. 2 to No. 4 can be used in most cases, and a No. 1 for large flounder. The illustrations on the following page show rigs for sole and flounder; multiple-hook rigs are illegal in B.C. and some other Pacific Coast waters, so check applicable provincial or state regulations before you go fishing.

Pre-tied bottomfish rigs are available from most tackle shops and mail-order catalogues.

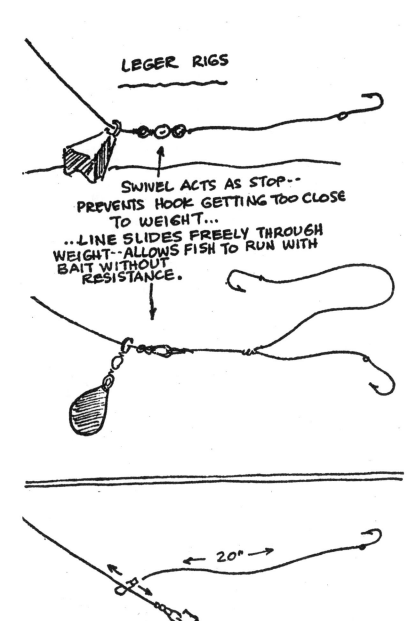

LEGER RIGS

SWIVEL ACTS AS STOP--
PREVENTS HOOK GETTING TOO CLOSE
TO WEIGHT...
..LINE SLIDES FREELY THROUGH
WEIGHT--ALLOWS FISH TO RUN WITH
BAIT WITHOUT
RESISTANCE.

← 20" →

Flatfish Techniques

Almost any rod and reel will work, but I prefer a light spinning outfit. The spinning reel allows the line to peel off quickly when it's dropped, and the light rod and line give sporty action when landing fish.

To start fishing, note the direction of wind and tide. Position your boat off to the side of your "hot spot" so wind and tide will carry you across it. Drop your lines to the bottom, then pull up six inches to a foot.

As the boat drifts over the area, raise and lower the rod slowly, bumping the bottom every few feet. You should get lots of active, sharp tugs as the flatfish grabs the bait. Set the hook with a short jerk, then reel in your fish!

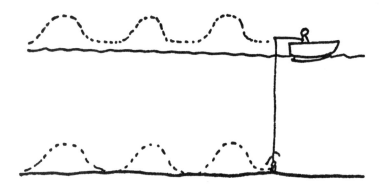

Small fish can be lifted aboard, but a small trout net is a good idea for larger specimens. Kill them with a sharp blow to the head, then store them in a cool, shady place. A picnic cooler or even a large bucket covered with a damp cloth will keep the fish firm and fresh.

Most of my personal experience with flatfish has been in deep water (over 100 feet), and I have found that a calm day at slack tide is most productive. If there is much wind or a strong tide, the boat moves too fast over the sole bed, and it is difficult to keep the bait on the bottom. In shallower areas, you can anchor over the spot and have good fishing in any reasonable weather or tide. Commercial net fishermen report having most success with flatfish at slack water conditions.

Depths for Finding Flatfish

Sole and flounder can be found in a wide range of depths, from just under the surface to depths of 1,500 to 2,000 feet!

Starry flounder often lie in shallow water off sandy shorelines. When trolling for coho in shallow water in early fall, I have often noticed flounder scurrying away from the approaching boat. When drifting over shallow sand bars looking for crabs, we have been startled by a sudden cloud of sand and mud as a big flounder rushes off from a position practically under our boat.

Flatfish often work their way in with a flooding tide, feeding on small crabs and other organisms very close to the water's edge. They work their way back out with the ebbing tide.

Flatfish tend to gather in groups over areas rich in nutrients and feed. These areas can be found at almost any depth, but 50 to 125 feet is probably a good range to work.

Generally speaking, the larger flatfish are in slightly deeper water than the smaller varieties. Some predatory species, like the big petrale sole, move around in search of small fish. I have caught sole weighing over six pounds in the midst of schools of small sand dabs.

All sole and flounder migrate to deeper water to spawn. They often begin moving down after the first fall storms in October or November. They spawn in late winter or early spring in deep water, then return to shallower water in April or May.

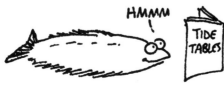

Trolling for Flounder

Large flounder can also be taken by a very slow troll or by motor mooching. A spinner and sea worm combination is the preferred bait. Strips of herring or other fish flesh are also effective.

Some of the rigs used for trout will work for flounder, but the multiple spinner "Willow-leaf" or "Gang-troll" arrangements offer too much drag and keep the line too shallow.

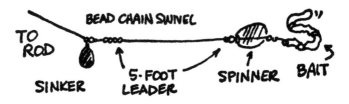

The bait should be very close to the bottom to get flounder. Slow rowing is an excellent way to troll, giving an erratic action to the lure as the boat moves ahead with each stroke.

Trolling with the motor in reverse will give a slower speed than in forward gear, as the boat moves against the resistance of the square stern.

Putting the motor in and out of gear is another method of slowing trolling speed.

On occasion, flounder will move up to mid-water areas to chase herring schools. Some fishermen get good catches of flounder off the central Oregon coast by trolling well off the bottom with whole herring or a herring strip. Some flounder are caught while trolling for salmon.

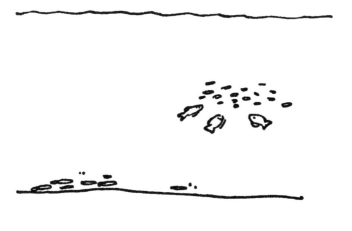

Chapter 4

HALIBUT

These are the largest of the flatfish, and many people consider them the best eating fish in the sea! They grow to enormous size—sport fishermen take many specimens weighing more than 100 pounds each year. Exceptional giants can exceed 200 pounds.

Halibut are tricky to catch. Generally speaking, they are found on large, flat, sand or mud banks off the open coast and in the Juan de Fuca Strait. They can be found in shallow inlets, or offshore hundreds of feet down.

Halibut are often found on the top of shallow banks surrounded by much deeper water. They prefer a sand or mud bottom, but inhabit these shallow reefs even if they are rocky.

Fisheries department personnel working on the Bowie Sea Mount near the Queen Charlotte Islands jigged for halibut on this rocky undersea mountain using chromed-lead Norwegian cod jigs. They were quite successful, getting fish of up to 200 pounds.

In southeast Alaska, huge halibut move into estuary areas off the river mouths when the salmon gather to spawn. Evidently, they catch and eat whole salmon, particularly pinks and sockeye. To these monsters, reputed to weigh as much as 500 pounds, even a ten-pound salmon is just a tasty tidbit.

Speaking of Alaska, there is a sign on the dock at the Alaskan capital city of Juneau that warns boaters not to bring large halibut aboard small boats. A number of accidents have occurred when large halibut, apparently played out, were dragged into small wooden boats. The halibut would suddenly thrash around and bang its powerful body and tail against the bottom and sides of the boat. Several boats have had their hull planking smashed open and gone down, with loss of life. The recommended procedure is to hook the fish to a strong towline with a heavy rubber shock absorber and tow it slowly to shore.

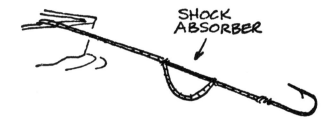

SHOCK
ABSORBER

If you still want to try for halibut after that story, get some heavy salmon tackle and at least 1,000 to 1,500 feet of heavy nylon line (perhaps 40-pound-test).

Halibut are carnivorous predators and will eat any live fish—herring, perch, rockfish, cod. Rig the bait alive on a large hook (see Chapter 6) and drift over the halibut grounds with the bait just off the bottom. Let the weight hit bottom frequently to be sure you are deep enough.

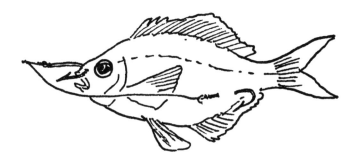

Halibut will also take many kinds of frozen bait. Commercial halibut fishermen use pieces of squid, octopus, herring, and true cod for bait on their set lines. Mooched whole herring or plug-cut herring is also very effective. Some anglers troll very slowly with the herring about three feet behind a big flasher.

As noted earlier, cod jigs and other artificial lures are used successfully for halibut. All jigging methods, using both natural and artificial bait, employ the basic technique of drifting over the selected area and bouncing the lures across the bottom.

After several years of research with our underwater camera, we were finally able to get the first-ever pictures of

halibut striking lures. They shied away from jigs more than two feet above the bottom. But when we jigged with the lure actually touching bottom, they attacked aggressively and inhaled the lure with a sucking motion. The lure disappeared in less than one-tenth of a second! (We show this exciting footage in our seminars and videos.)

For more detailed information on catching halibut, and the research results from our latest experiments with halibut, see my book *Quick Tips for Catching Halibut!*

Chapter 5

ROCKFISH

Rockfish populations in some areas of British Columbia have declined to the point that fishing for them is prohibited. Rockfish generally do not migrate very far, but stay in one general area all their lives, sometimes 30 years or more.

The reefs and kelp beds where they live are often in protected areas where we can fish them in any weather and at any time of the year. They are usually eager biters on a variety of lures, so they have become more and more a target species. As it gets tougher to catch salmon, rockfish are getting more fishing pressure than the populations can handle.

TYPICAL ROCKFISH

If you can practise catch and release, so much the better. At the very least, take only enough for one meal. Rockfish are at their best in the first few hours after they are caught.

There are at least fifteen different varieties of rockfish (often called rock cod) along the North Pacific coast. The fish have air bladders that allow them to hang motionless in the water a few feet above a rocky bottom.

They will attack any shiny lure, feather jig, or natural herring bait that is dragged past them. While they will also feed on clams, pile worms, etc., it is easier to attract them with a slow-moving shiny bait or lure.

Most rockfish tend to hang in schools in one rocky area and will not venture far in search of food. The black rockfish and yellow-tailed rockfish (sometimes called sea bass) are exceptions to this rule. They are roving, mid-water fish that cover wide areas in search of food. These active, sporty fish will strike trolled lures readily, and many have been taken on bucktail flies. If you happen on a school of these fish, you can have great sport if you stop your boat and cast small lures into the school. They will strike aggressively and put up a strong fight. In many ways, they look and fight like freshwater bass.

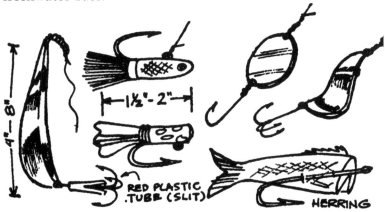

4"- 8"

1½" - 2"

RED PLASTIC
TUBE (SLIT)

HERRING

A very effective method of catching the bottom-dwelling varieties of rockfish is to drift slowly over a rocky bottom. Most productive areas are often near reefs or along rocky shorelines. The fish often gather in large schools around underwater features such as shipwrecks, junked cars, rocks, and reefs. Many people catch them casting from breakwaters. Fishing along the edge of kelp beds—or even right in them— is also productive.

Drop your line until it hits bottom, then pull up about five or six feet. Let your boat drift slowly with the wind or tide over the rocky area or along the kelp bed. Work your rod up and down to give the lure a darting, erratic action. Two quick jerks followed by slack line to let the lure flutter down is a procedure used by many commercial cod fishermen.

The key to providing proper action is to use sharp, erratic jerks to attract the fish, then the slower flutter (or even hanging still momentarily) to allow the fish to grab the lure.

Every minute or two, you should let out line until it hits bottom, then reposition it five or six feet up. This will keep the lure near the bottom as you drift over areas of varying

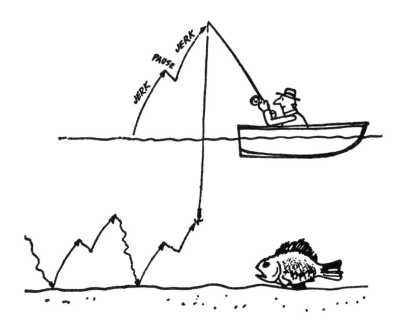

depth. You will probably find one spot in your drift where you get most of your strikes. If this is the case, keep making short drifts over this area or anchor just on the uptide side and let your lure drift into the productive spot.

Another method for catching black rockfish is used by our artist, Nelson Dewey, who learned from an experienced fisherman friend. (A good way to learn any type of fishing is to ask the local experts, who are usually more than willing to

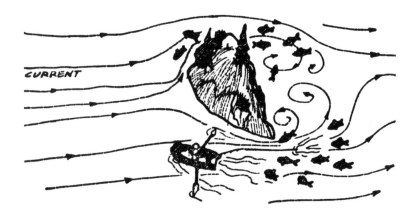

share their knowledge.) Toward evening, he rows his dinghy into a partially sheltered bay with a good tidal flow. By rowing against the current and slightly faster, he "trolls" a line through the back eddies where the fish seem to congregate to feed. He uses small feathered plugs with little or no weight. At dusk the fish will often come to the surface (apparently to feed) and jump! In the semi-darkness, it's difficult to see them, but a weightless lure trolled six to ten feet behind the boat, just below the surface, will usually bring a good catch.

(Note: Be sure to have a good flashlight for finding your way back to shore and for warning off other boats!)

Chapter 6
LINGCOD

Lingcod frequent rocky areas with strong tidal movement. These voracious feeders do not have an air bladder and lie motionless on the rocky bottom, waiting for their prey. When a darting, erratic bait comes near, they explode from their hiding place and viciously attack the bait, often swallowing it completely. They put up a dogged, determined fight.

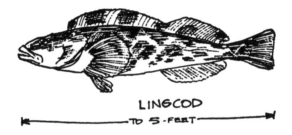

LINGCOD
TO 5-FEET

Lingcod grow quite large. Twenty- to 30-pound fish are not uncommon, and some monsters exceed 50 pounds.

The large lings are often caught using rockfish for bait! Sometimes when playing a rockfish (or sole or flounder), the line will suddenly stop jerking and you'll feel only a heavy pull on the line. If you haven't snagged the bottom or some kelp, a large lingcod has probably grabbed hold of your rockfish.

You can bring both fish to the boat with a firm, steady reeling in of line. When they are close to the boat, do not lift them partially out of the water, or the ling will let go. If you quietly slip a net under them, or gaff the ling (the rockfish is already hooked), you will have two fish, the ling probably a large specimen.

If you want to catch large ling, use a live rockfish or sole for bait. Rig two of the largest hooks you have, one through the snout and the other through the side back at the anal fin.

Let the fish swim freely, and it will head straight for the bottom. Keep it just off the rocks by raising and lowering the rod. This will keep the fish from hiding in a crevice. Use only about two to four ounces of weight (or none at all if it is not too deep).

Chapter 7

RED SNAPPER

This member of the rockfish family lives at greater depths than any of its relatives. It is seldom caught less than 60 or 70 feet deep, and commercial catches are made at 600 to 700 feet down in offshore areas

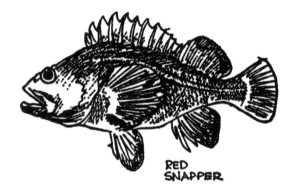

RED
SNAPPER

Red snapper can be taken on the same type of lure as other rockfish. Any shiny lure, feather jig, or herring bait will bring a solid strike if bounced within the sight of a hungry snapper—and it seems they are always hungry!

They have very large mouths, so you might experiment with larger baits to see if this method will catch larger fish. (As I explain in my book *How to Catch Salmon: Basic*

Fundamentals, federal fisheries department experiments showed that large lures caught the biggest chinook salmon.)

When you bring up a snapper from deep water, its air bladder will be puffed up so large that the whole fish is bloated. The air bladder will often push some of the internal organs right up into the fish's mouth.

Snapper can grow quite large. Twenty-pounders are not uncommon. They are delicious eating; some people claim the white flaky meat tastes similar to crab.

Chapter 8

FISHING THE REEFS
FOR ROCKFISH AND LINGCOD

By Sidney S. Girling

This chapter deals with fishing rockfish and lingcod off the reefs near Victoria. It is a remarkable story written by a remarkable gentleman, the late Sidney Girling. He fished these reefs from a rowboat until he was 85.

His theories on vertical jigging with lures designed especially for this purpose have proven extremely effective, as he outlines in his excellent chapter. Serious bottomfishing devotees will find Girling's material absorbing and valuable; newcomers to bottomfishing will find his methods simple and effective.

Although some of the material is now dated, it is still generally applicable, and his octopus lure design has stood the test of time. The historical view Girling provides is interesting, and it is a delight to read his philosophy of fishing and his comments on fishing with children.

—C.W.

Why Do It?

There must be many people living on our extensive rocky coastline—and boaters on cruising craft with rockfish actually under their "doorstep"—who would be glad to supplement their food supply with excellent fresh fish at short notice and little cost.

But first, why rockfish? Why not salmon? In fact, why go fishing at all? One is bound to go shopping sometime, and there is plenty of good fish in the stores.

Why go to all the trouble of painting the boat, fixing the tackle, rowing to the reef, catching the slimy, spiny creatures, and filleting and disposing of the remains when any commercial fisherman will gladly do all this for you?

It could be said of most hobbies that the material product of our labour could be much more easily obtained in the stores. Possibly the reason some of us enjoy our hobbies and the work they entail is that the urge to engage in such productive activities is as much a part of us as our hands and brains. We are satisfying an inner compulsion that for over two million years was partly responsible for our survival.

Throughout the greater part of that vast stretch of time, those defective individuals who lacked that urge and lay abed dreaming the happy hours away may have had offspring, but they were less likely to survive to perpetuate their parents' deficiency. So it came about that this subconscious desire became part of our make-up.

However, very late in that two-million-year span, when civilization was invented, some perceptive individuals managed to survive very well indeed by inducing others to do the physical work for them. It appears they may have produced descendants who do not get emotional satisfaction when engaged in such productive activities as making handicrafts, gardening, etc. In fact, they look upon them as chores.

But there are still, in these days of highrise apartments and supermarkets, many fortunate people who have, and are

in a position to satisfy, that inborn instinct to produce at least some small part of their physical needs by their own efforts. Such endeavour is good for the soul. It may be cooking, dressmaking, gardening, winemaking, beekeeping, hunting, fishing, tacklemaking, art, or handicrafts of various kinds.

The material products of these activities can be purchased in the supermarkets, but the spiritual satisfaction derived from one's own achievement cannot be bought anywhere, at any price.

In past years I have engaged in all of these activities, except dressmaking, but this writing is about rockfishing, which I have found to be most beneficial physically and emotionally and, compared to salmon fishing, more consistently profitable. The end product is more palatable to many people. For those fortunate anglers who have learned to use their hands, making tackle and lures gives them these benefits plus a financial gain.

With many hobbies, there are operations essential to completing the project that one would gladly skip—in the case of fishing, filleting the fish and disposing of the remains. However, it's good for the psyche to determine to do it yourself and not leave the unpleasant work to others.

If the writing that follows seems to downgrade salmon and salmon fishing, it is to awaken saltwater anglers to the merits of reef fishing once you have lures as clean and efficient as those used in salmon fishing.

Many salmon fishermen say that for food, they prefer freshly caught rockfish or lingcod over salmon. My wife and I agree, but I repeat, freshly caught! Even a few days' delay makes a difference. Cold storage gives us good sustenance, but the fine flavour is lost and sometimes a new one is

BOTTOMFISH
HERE:
8:15 AM TUES
8:50 AM WED
9:25 AM THUR.

acquired. Bought fillets are never as good as freshly caught, unless, of course, the bought fillets are freshly caught.

To be sure, catch the fish yourself or get your youngsters to get them for you. Once you get to know where, how, and when to fish, a catch is fairly certain.

This cannot be said of salmon fishing, even if you get out of your warm bed before dawn, that unearthly hour that is the best time to get good salmon and prove you have intestinal fortitude.

I have done this and had good fishing, but at my age I prefer to be out in the warm sunshine after a good meal. Those lovely, calm, sunny days are not the best days for salmon fishing.

The female of the species instinctively expects the male to return from the hunt with something for the family to eat. Usually, she is not too concerned about the sporting angle.

I recall the following incident because it shows that the subconscious feelings implanted in us before civilization came into being still influence our reactions. It was, I believe, in the summer of 1953, on one of those lovely Victoria days of clear sky, bright sunshine, and no wind, that my wife and I went fishing from Brentwood Bay on the Saanich Inlet. We fished around Senanus Island, getting rockfish and sole, and then, on our way back, we landed a large flounder near the boathouse.

As we unloaded the fish onto the float, two ladies from a fishing party that had pulled in ahead of us stopped to look at the fish. I heard one say, "The boys said there were no fish in the inlet."

I shall never forget those words and the way in which she said them—as if the fish we had were just as acceptable to her as the fish the "boys" said were not there. There were plenty of good fish in the inlet, but not the kind they were fishing for.

Now, in my 88th year, I feel an enjoyable part of my life would be wasted if I did not pass on to others the knowledge acquired during many years of fishing, from my experience with sticklebacks in a pond in Essex, England, 1899, to a 49-pound lingcod, 1969, to bigger fish that got away.

Fishing From Shore

Through the 1930s, I landed many rockfish and lingcod by casting from the shore, using wooden plugs I had made from cedar boughs because plug casualties were high and it was fun to make my own.

To reach the fish, the plug must move near the bottom, so it is likely it will get snagged. A spincasting outfit is not strong enough to pull free, so it is better to use a stiffer casting rod with a free-spool casting reel and fifteen-pound nylon at least.

The most productive fishing was from the Ogden Point breakwater between late winter and spring, when the kelp had disappeared, starting an hour after sunset and continuing into the night. We often stayed until ten o'clock. The fish—black rockfish (commonly called black bass)—feed on the surface after dark, travelling in schools along the shoreline and occasionally splashing. Rarely did we come away empty-handed.

If, some calm evening, you are standing on a rocky shore in the near-dark and you hear an occasional splash, it is most likely the black rockfish feeding. They do not bite in rough or phosphorescent water.

We found the most effective lure to be a strip of fresh pork rind, the thinner the better, salted to preserve and whiten it, then cut to resemble a small fish about two and a half inches long. Punch a hole in the "head" with the point of a sharp knife and hang the lure on a 1-0 hook, free to wiggle. Clamp one-third of an ounce of lead on the nylon about eight inches from the hook. More weight will sink the lure too deep.

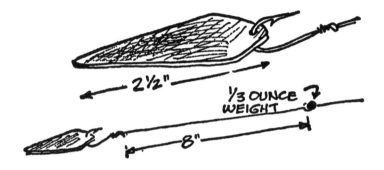

Cast it out about 70 feet and retrieve it while jerking the rod tip occasionally. This bait is so tough that one piece will land many fish, and spares kept in a jar with wet salt will keep for years (twenty, to my knowledge) and still take fish.

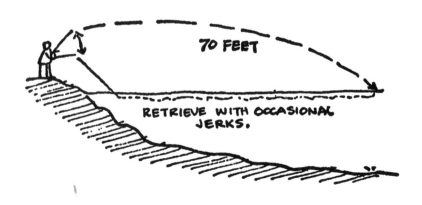

There being no spincasting reels in the '30s, and because a free-spool reel will not cast one-third of an ounce, we cast with no reel, dropping the line at our feet. A spincasting outfit would be much better.

The fish may also be taken after dark, fly-fishing with a white streamer fly. This can be done from a wharf, boat, or rocky point.

We usually landed more than could be eaten fresh, so, having no fridge, we dressed the surplus fillets with smoked salt and hung them up to dry. This to my taste is better than freezing. Smoked fillets make a nice change and are excellent for fishcakes.

Bottomfish: A Sure Thing

In the daytime, black rockfish schools swim deeper. Using rubber lures, I have taken large ones from the bottom, over 100 feet down. I've also caught them by trolling with salmon lures at various depths off rocky points. The problem with the latter is finding the right spot and depth, the same as it is with salmon fishing, but with one difference: If you note tide conditions when you get one fish, you will likely find them near the same spot and depth day after day. When the tide turns, they will likely be on the other side of the point.

We all know that getting salmon is a game of chance. Possibly, that is one reason it is so popular. As with gambling,

if you are lucky the reward may be big. With experience, you may increase your chances of success, but with salmon fishing you can never approach the degree of certainty attainable when fishing for rockfish.

Salmon are rovers—here today, gone tomorrow—feeding at unpredictable times and in unpredictable areas and depths. On the contrary, fish living on the reefs are there all day and every day (provided they are not fished out). Lingcod move to shallower water to spawn, but they are back to deep water and their lairs before March.

Not only are bottomfish an excellent food, but they also provide dependable outdoor entertainment. There is a great variety of fish species. From an area the size of four city blocks, I have taken six species of rockfish—copper, quillback, black, orange, red snapper, and vermilion— lingcod, cabezon, marbled sculpin, dogfish, kelp greenling, white spotted greenling, and rock, sand, and flathead soles. All were caught on vertically operated rubber lures, and all are edible. I lost a fish that sped off into deeper water; it felt like a streetcar, but was likely a large halibut. I kept tightening the brake, but there was no stopping the fish. After many yards of line had run out, the twenty-pound nylon broke.

Lingcod Techniques

Bottomfish behave very differently than salmon do. A small lingcod, up to ten pounds or so, will fight to get free, but the large ones make no attempt to run. They appear somewhat insensitive to pain or fear.

Frequently I've hooked a rockfish of about three pounds 100 feet down, more or less, and in a few seconds there is a dead stop to raising the fish. You wonder if it has holed in, or if the sinker snagged in the rocks. Then you feel a slow movement, and you can guess that a large lingcod has taken hold of the fish.

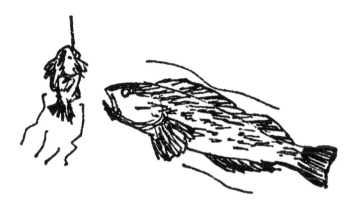

As you raise it, the lingcod bears down with its large pectoral fins but does not move forward. It is a heavy, dead-weight pull to bring the fish to the surface, alternately holding the line and raising the rod with all the force the rod will bear, then lowering the rod while reeling in the slack. Oddly, the fish makes no attempt to go down in the interval when the pressure is eased.

1. RAISE ROD - KEEP LINE FROM RUNNING OUT.

2. QUICKLY LOWER ROD, WINDING IN LINE AT SAME TIME. TAKE UP SLACK. REPEAT 1-2-1-2 ETC.

Eventually, on the surface, it will lie there motionless with its jaws across the rockfish while you wonder what to do next. Unlike a large salmon, which is finished when brought to the

boat side, the lingcod has not started to fight. It seems unaware of the danger it is in, despite having been forced up from the dim depths and a pressure of 50 pounds per square inch to bright sunlight, no pressure, and a boat nearby.

A rockfish brought up from that depth fights most of the way up, then floats helplessly on the surface, unable to descend because of its greatly distended air sac. Not so the lingcod. It lies there, not from gas in its stomach or loss of physical strength, but apparently from mental dullness and obstinacy. Down below, the lingcod is lord of all it surveys, and no one is going to take that rockfish from it. The older and larger the lingcod gets, the more obstinate it becomes.

I've had three experiences of this nature. In the first two, the lingcod were not as large as in the third, and they let go upon reaching the surface. The third lingcod was much larger, around 50 pounds, and it lay motionless on the surface, holding on to its, or my, rockfish. I gaffed it under the lower jaw. It apparently felt nothing whatsoever, for it made no movement nor showed any sign of discomfort. It was when I started to lift it that the fish went berserk, threw water all over me, bent the gaff, and made off!

I did most of my fishing from a small boat or from a larger one with a cockpit too small to share with a large and lively lingcod. After the episode just described, I always carried a

towline in the tackle box. It was made up of a large hook attached to a strong line with a length of rubber to cushion a sudden jerk. A large fish could then be towed to a beach and safely landed. Think twice before you gaff a large lingcod or halibut from a small boat.

Anyone who has handled a rockfish and been pricked by one of the many sharp spines on its dorsal fin knows how painful it can be. It seems to me that a fish that can swallow a live rockfish has little feeling in its mouth, throat, or stomach.

One large lingcod that seized my rockfish let go when I tried

to hook it with the towline. It then made repeated splashing attacks on the fish lying on the surface, three feet from the boat, trying to get it by the head in order to swallow it. The ling must have been pricked, but it showed no sign. After several tries it gave up and leisurely submerged.

On another occasion, I had nearly all the fish we needed when a lingcod grabbed what was to have been the last fish. Pulling it to the surface, I tapped it lightly on the head to make it let go, but I had to give it a harder blow before it would leave.

Again, in the summer of 1968, I was reeling in after a bite when a large lingcod took hold. Upon getting it to the surface, all I could see was a small part of the rubber squid projecting from its jaws, so I presumed that the ling was hooked to my rod line. After a short attempt to tow it to shore, the ling disgorged a four-and-three-quarter-pound lingcod, likely one of its own offspring, that was hooked to the squid, and I netted it.

Four days later the same thing happened, possibly with the same fish. This time there was no sign of the lure; the line was coming straight from the fish's tightly closed jaws. Again, I thought it must be hooked. I put the rod in the rod rest and had towed the fish a considerable distance toward shore when the line slackened, and I reeled in an unconscious five-pound lingcod bearing the tooth marks of its elder.

Fishing with Young People

I feel here that I must speak up for the young people. I have always felt it unwise and even unkind to take them salmon fishing for their first fishing experience. I would not exchange my early adventures with sticklebacks and small roach for many of the salmon trips taken since. They are happy memories of quiet ponds and small streams, moorhens, kingfishers, and water rats; butterflies, dragonflies, swallows, and great expectations. These small adventures are appreciated only when one is young; to miss them then is to miss them forever.

Salmon fishing is for grown-ups. They can sit still for hours, expecting something big to happen. Young people like smaller events happening more frequently.

The boat goes on and on, hour after hour. Dad says, "Can't you keep still—do you have to keep moving around?" For the older ones, it's a welcome rest, for the younger, a bore. The

young ones get more excitement lying on a wharf trying to get the shiners they can see below. They might be even happier if their dad took part. He will find it takes knowledge and attention to catch shiners and to hold the love and respect of children.

My wife, Marjorie, got interested in fishing in this way. On our first fishing trip together, she brought along cushions and a book. I intended to get rockfish or lingcod, and the only baits I knew of then were the natural ones, so I tied the boat to the pilings of a wharf to catch shiners. Shiners are not easy to hook. You can watch them getting the bait off the hook, but landing them takes experience. After watching my futile attempts for a while, Marjorie said, "Let me try," and that was it—she was hooked.

Salmon trolling and drifting for rockfish each have their pleasures and drawbacks. Trolling for salmon is restful: the motor purrs (I hope) while you sit back enjoying the sunshine and scenery, the gulls, ducks, and divers. If you're lucky, there'll be an interval of excitement when you land a fish.

Driftfishing calls for constant attention every minute, keeping contact with the rough, rocky contours below. A little

inattention, and you may get snagged. With the slowly drifting boat there is no engine noise, just quietness and a feeling of expectation and mild excitement. Of the two kinds of entertainment, the latter is most appealing to the young. There is constant action that they can take part in, and with skill and experience there is a 10 to 1 chance or better of getting fish. This, to the young, is the purpose of fishing.

Girling's Secrets

When I retired, we kept fishing records for fifteen years, listing the date, area, number, species, and weights of all fish caught. The average number of reef fish caught per trip nearly doubled in that time, and the fruitless trips were reduced from 1 in 4 (the average for the first eight years) to 1 in 30 (the average for the last seven years). I should mention that in the first eight years, much time was spent salmon trolling and fishing with natural baits.

In the last seven years, making an average of 26 trips per year from March to November, there were only two blank days in one year, one blank day in each of four years, and no blank days in two years. Rubber imitations of squid or octopus were used exclusively.

Of 24 trips made during 1969, the last full year of fishing, there were no blank days and 17 lingcod and 57 rockfish were taken. The total weight of fish taken was 452¾ pounds, an average of 18.8 pounds per trip, which would yield about six and a half pounds of fillets. A lingcod yields a full third of its weight in fillets without skin or bones, a rockfish slightly less than one third.

On some trips only one fish was taken, but more often than not we stopped fishing when one large or four to five smaller ones were landed. We kept enough fillets for three meals for my wife and I, and some for neighbours who in turn gave us fruit and vegetables.

We did not freeze any fish, believing it better to leave them in the sea and get them fresh when needed.

Being retired, it was possible to go out any time in the week when conditions were right, and many times we took all the fish we needed within an hour. This greatly increased catch over former years was due to six factors:

1. not spending time on salmon;
2. not using fishing time to get natural bait;
3. using vertically operated rubber imitations of squid and octopus, properly rigged;
4. fishing in deeper water;

5. finding unknown rocky outcrops in a large area of mud and fixing their positions by observing and recording landmarks; and
6. discovering that rockfish in some areas feed on the rising tide while others, maybe only a few hundred yards away, feed on the falling tide.

No doubt many experienced anglers have discovered this last fact, but I have never seen it mentioned in the few books available that deal with rockfish.

It is well known that fish in a stream lie in the eddy behind boulders, darting out into the flowing water to capture passing food and then returning to their resting place. Apparently. dwellers among the rocks on the sea bottom also do this.

Where a rocky point runs out from the shore into deep water and the tide flows over it, most fish will be found feeding on the lee side of the ridge; this holds true for rocky islands and any rocky prominence on the sea bottom. It is fortunate that this is so: where the fish are feeding, the boat is drifting

from high ground to lower, meaning the chances of getting snagged are much less than if one drifts from low to high ground. To make it more clear, most fish living on one side of an undersea prominence feed on the rising tide, and fish on the other side feed on a falling tide—in both cases, they are sheltered from the flowing water.

This is not to say that no fish will be caught when drifting over a rising sea bottom. Some may be taken, but not nearly so many.

My experience is that fish living around rocks do not strike when the water is stationary, high or low, or when it is moving

at a speed that makes it difficult for them to maintain contact with the bottom. A moderate tidal movement is best, rising or falling. We don't know whether this is because the fish are too sedentary to face fast water or because the rubber squid tentacles do not behave in a lifelike manner in fast water. Heavier sinkers and weighted lures might work. The lure should drop head first, after the sinker strikes bottom.

If you're fishing around a small island, the fish along the sides will be found feeding during a moderate current. When the speed of the current increases they stop, but may still be found to bite in the lee of the island.

I have presumed that rockfish in other areas behave as they do in the area of Haro Strait, where I fished. There, a wide rocky point pushes out from the shoreline and runs

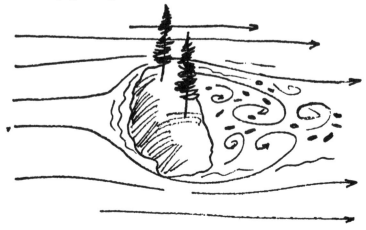

downward under water, forming a mound that projects a quarter-mile out into water 120 feet deep. It is mainly covered with mud, but scattered rocky outcrops were located by drifting and feeling the bottom with the sinker. An uneven bottom, or hooking a fish, indicates a rocky outcrop. The position of these outcrops was at once fixed by observing fixed objects on land or water.

The most likely areas to search for rocks were determined by subdividing the spaces between soundings on the chart and drawing in the depth lines so found. Where the lines are closer together, indicating a steeper slope, there is a greater chance of finding rock.

It pays to have a chart of the area to be fished and a tide book. These are inexpensive and can be obtained at most marine outlets. Time of tide is important for determining feeding times and varies greatly from station to station where tide recordings are made.

Most charts show depth lines at three, six, ten, and twenty fathoms. To know, when out on the water, where you are in relation to these lines on the chart, cut the reel line at these four points, measuring from the sinker, and tie it together again with blood (twist) knots. As the line runs out, the knots can be counted with a finger. A further help is to paint the knots with different colours of enamel.

The most productive fishing is from a boat, drifting with the tide in water 60 to 120 feet or more deep. You can use handlines with heavier sinkers, but a short stiff rod about

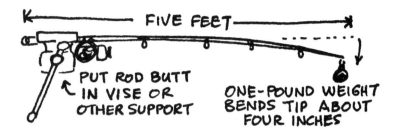

FIVE FEET

PUT ROD BUTT
IN VISE OR
OTHER SUPPORT

ONE-POUND WEIGHT
BENDS TIP ABOUT
FOUR INCHES

five feet in length with a free spool and multiplying reel of the bay-fishing type is much more satisfactory.

When the rod I use is fastened in a horizontal position, a one-pound weight hung from the top ring deflects the tip four inches from the horizontal; this is the stiffness recommended.

In the last nine years of boat fishing, I have taken 2,540 pounds of rockfish, lingcod, and salmon on homemade lures and a rod made from seasoned spiraea (*Spiraea discolor*), a common shrub around Victoria. This wood, when seasoned for a year, is much like cane, strong and springy. My rod was made from solid spiraea wood, cut from a large stem, but a good rod can be made from a suitable shoot, five feet long and a full half-inch in diameter at the butt. Cut the shoot in the fall, season it, and, if necessary, straighten it with steam. Slip eighteen inches of old rubber garden hose over the butt. Use two hose clamps to hold the reel, and fasten on the rod rings (made or bought) with adhesive tape.

The rod must be fairly stiff to feel and follow the very uneven bottom while drifting on the tide with a six-ounce sinker. A flexible rod does not give as good action to the lure

RUBBER HOSE BUTT
ON SPIRAEA
ROD.

nor transmit sufficiently well the feel of the bottom. When a sudden rise is encountered, it will not raise the weight quickly enough to avoid snagging. When a large rockfish bites, it must be lifted immediately and held or it may hole in; this a flexible rod cannot do.

Trolling and casting rods are usually operated from 45 degrees to vertical. When driftfishing, hold the rod horizontally when the sinker is on the ground, adjusting the reel to keep it so as the depth changes. Hooking and lifting a fish may raise the rod to around 45 degrees, but never vertical.

Since the reel is positioned on trolling rods some distance from the butt, it is rather far from the body when horizontal. A shortened butt is more comfortable. An overall length of five feet is recommended, especially in a dinghy.

The salmon angler who wants to get rockfish or lingcod when the salmon are not biting can use his trolling rod as it is by running the line through the lower rings and dropping it out through a ring one or two short of the tip. If used frequently in this way, the ring from which the line drops should be replaced with a porcelain one to save wear on the line.

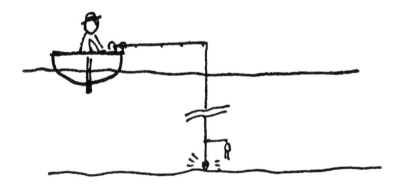

A salmon-trolling rod can be made stiff enough by cutting the tip back until it passes the stiffness test recommended and then relocating the rings.

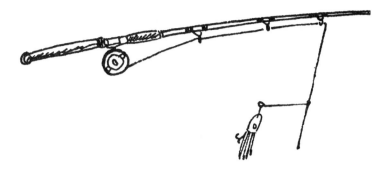

Bait

Over the years I have used every kind of bait except live bait. It may be the most effective, if it stays alive, but I prefer to get the food with a minimum of suffering. True, small fish get eaten by larger, and they in turn by us, but to force a captive small fish with a hook through its back alone into what it knows is an extremely dangerous area to be killed or to eventually die trying to escape is unnecessary cruelty.

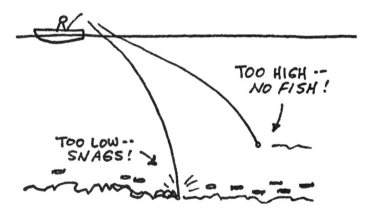

Most small fish, like birds in flocks, move in schools for protection—there are more eyes to spot enemies. If there are 100 fish in a school, an individual has a 99 to 1 chance of not getting eaten by the first bite of a predator. A small fish tethered alone lives in fear. Nature is brutal and we are part of it, but I see no reason to be brutal if it can be avoided. In this case, it can be.

Most people like to see fish free in the water but also as food on the table. The unavoidable action in between should be cut to a minimum. Always take a club along to dispatch the fish quickly. It is a less protracted death than being eaten alive, its most likely fate.

A serviceable club and hook extractor can be made from a fifteen-inch-long, seasoned spiraea shoot of a diameter that will fit tightly into a five-inch length of half-inch galvanized iron water pipe. The pipe should be secured with a wedge in a saw cut at one end, and the other end of the wood tapered, flattened, and notched to engage the hook.

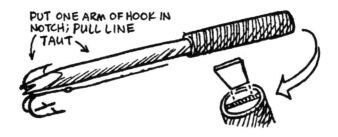

PUT ONE ARM OF HOOK IN NOTCH; PULL LINE TAUT

To be effective, frozen herring or any other natural bait must be used fresh. They may not be on hand when needed; take time to get (time that could be better spent catching fish); and cannot be used twice. Worst of all, because dogfish hunt by smell, and bottomfish by sight, the likelihood of getting dogfish instead of rockfish is much increased. They will follow the scent of blood, stale fish, or worms from a considerable distance. I doubt they would investigate the smell of rubber, although they *will* take hold if they see a rubber lure in action.

SNIF! SNIF!

Dogfish are very good fried or boiled and made into fishcakes. Westerners are prejudiced. Our dog was not—quite the contrary.

Considering the abundance of bottomfish in our waters, it is astonishing that there is so little specialized gear for capturing them available in our local stores. The rods displayed are much too long and flexible for bottomfishing in deep water, where the larger fish are. They are useful for fishing from shore or from a boat in water less than 40 feet deep, where casting is the best method. Using the very numerous horizontally operated lures, much gear is lost because of the horizontal movement and the necessity of getting close to the bottom.

Driftfishing with vertically operated lures is not so productive in depths of less than 30 feet. It is likely that the boat's being close, above the lure, puts the fish off feeding. At greater depths the boat is not so visible nor so threatening. Some fish can be taken by casting well away from the boat into water the boat has not passed over.

I believe I am right in saying that almost all of the exceedingly numerous lures displayed in local stores are

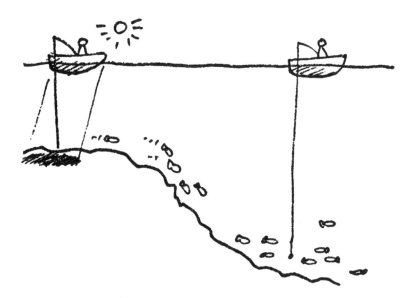

designed solely for trolling or casting horizontally, so are not very efficient in a deep-water vertical drop.

The two exceptions are Mike's Snagless Cod Jigger and the Norwegian plated-lead cod jig. These are good. I once hooked a very large halibut on one off James Island. It took half an hour to get it to the surface and it looked to weigh as much as me, but it broke away after over an hour's battling.

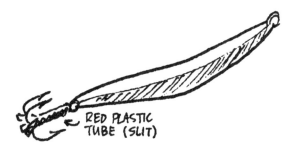

RED PLASTIC
TUBE (SLIT)

During this incident, I learned that the towline should have included a length of rubber in its make-up. I hooked the fish with the towline, but it dived down and snapped the strong line, which was tied to a cleat. Fortunately, it was not a small boat.

The drawback to this cod jig is that the hooks unavoidably strike bottom, catch weeds, and snag on rocks. They must be raised frequently to check for weeds. This, in deep water, takes time that could be better employed catching fish. It is not pleasing to wonder how many fish you passed with a weedy lure.

Trolling for bottomfish is far less satisfactory than driftfishing or casting. When you're trolling, the lure snags if it is too deep. And if it's less deep, it misses most of the fish, as only the high spots are fished.

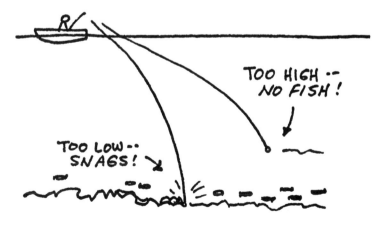

As already mentioned, casting is a fairly good way to get bottomfish when you're fishing in water less than 40 feet deep. The lures available (Buzz-Bombs, plugs, spoons, etc.) are effective, but when fishing in water more than 40 feet deep, drifting on the tide with the line as vertical as the current will allow is more productive. Use lures, rigging, and sinkers designed for vertical action in deep water on a rough bottom, and you will get larger fish and more of them, with less loss of tackle, than you will casting in the shallower water.

The Best Lure

The lures I found best of all were close imitations of squid or octopus, a favourite food of all rock-dwellers. The important feature is the tentacles. The lifelike movement caused by the up and down motion of the lure seems very attractive to the fish. I once hooked a good-sized lingcod on a rubber squid. As it came to the surface, it spat out a small octopus. While dressing it, I found two more in its distended stomach. My lure was the fourth.

After trying many materials for an imitation squid or octopus, including lifelike imitations of Pacific squid made with latex rubber, the best on all points for the amateur craftsman was the finger of a rubber glove, large size for deep water and smaller for where smaller fish are.

The colour is not important. Squid and octopus can change colour quickly from dull white to dark red. I have had equal success with near-white, yellow, pink, and red. This lure really simulates a small octopus.

A pair of gloves will give material for ten lures (about ten cents each). To restore the roundness of the fingers when

they have been flattened by storage, fill the glove with very hot water, followed by cold.

The following drawing illustrates the only tools essential to make the lures.

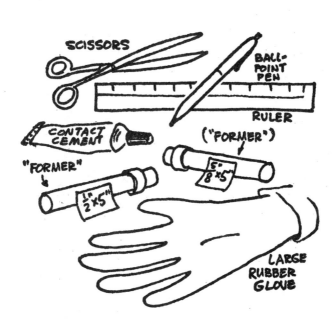

How to Make Girling's Octopus Lure

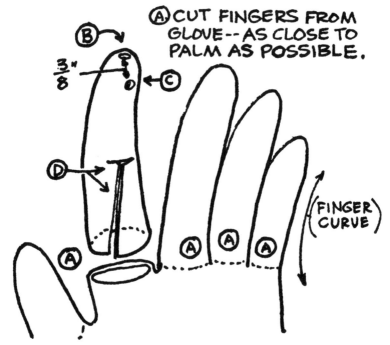

Ⓐ CUT FINGERS FROM GLOVE -- AS CLOSE TO PALM AS POSSIBLE.

$\frac{3}{8}$"

FINGER CURVE

PUNCH HOLES Ⓑ & Ⓒ IN EACH FINGER AS SHOWN -- ON CONCAVE SIDE (INSIDE CURVE). USE ⅛" DIAMETER HOLLOW PUNCH -- OR CUT WITH TIP OF SCISSORS. Ⓑ MUST BE AN OPEN HOLE TO LET AIR OUT. Ⓒ CAN BE A SLIT.

PUNCH HOLE OR SLIT Ⓓ HALFWAY FROM TIP TO BASE. THEN CUT SLIT FROM BASE TO HOLE

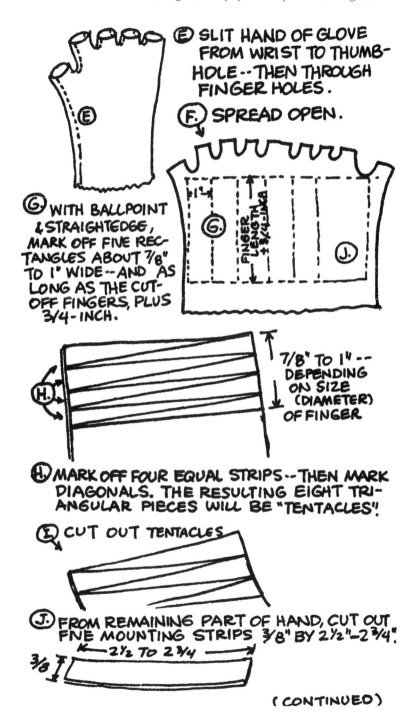

E SLIT HAND OF GLOVE FROM WRIST TO THUMB-HOLE -- THEN THROUGH FINGER HOLES.

F. SPREAD OPEN.

G WITH BALLPOINT & STRAIGHTEDGE, MARK OFF FIVE RECTANGLES ABOUT 7/8" TO 1" WIDE -- AND AS LONG AS THE CUT-OFF FINGERS, PLUS 3/4-INCH.

FINGER LENGTH + 3/4-INCH

7/8" TO 1" -- DEPENDING ON SIZE (DIAMETER) OF FINGER

H. MARK OFF FOUR EQUAL STRIPS -- THEN MARK DIAGONALS. THE RESULTING EIGHT TRIANGULAR PIECES WILL BE "TENTACLES"!

I. CUT OUT TENTACLES

J. FROM REMAINING PART OF HAND, CUT OUT FIVE MOUNTING STRIPS 3/8" BY 2½"-2¾".

3/8

2½ TO 2¾

(CONTINUED)

OCTOPUS LURE (CONT.)

(K) WRAP A MOUNTING STRIP AROUND A "FORMER" OF APPROPRIATE SIZE. OVERLAP & GLUE ENDS TOGETHER.

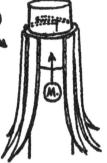

(L) CEMENT EIGHT TENTACLES TO MOUNTING STRIP AS SHOWN. BEFORE GLUEING, STRETCH & RELEASE ONE TENTACLE. IT SHOULD SHOW A DEFINITE CURVE. ATTACH TENTACLES SO THEY CURVE OUTWARDS.

(M) SPACE TENTACLES TO LEAVE A GAP 180° FROM WHERE STRIP OVERLAPS.

(N) WITH PEN, MAKE A MARK ON MOUNTING STRIP BETWEEN 4th & 5th TENTACLES (AT OVERLAP) -- AND ON FINGER AT 180° FROM SLIT (D).

(O) APPLY CEMENT TO TENTACLES (SHADED AREAS) AND INSIDE OF FINGER -- TO CORRESPOND. DO NOT WAIT FOR CONTACT CEMENT TO DRY!

(P.) IMMEDIATELY JOIN FINGER TO TENTACLES. LINE UP MARKS ON MOUNTING STRIP AND FINGER. WORK BOTH WAYS FROM THERE. OVERLAP & CEMENT FINGER 180° FROM MARKS.

FINGER

MOUNTING STRIP

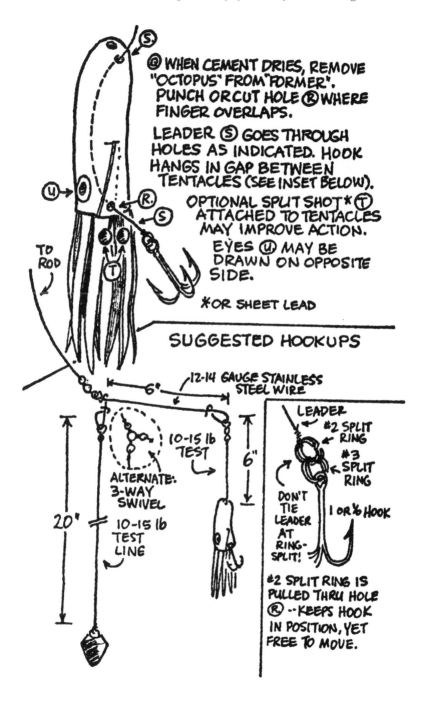

ⓐ WHEN CEMENT DRIES, REMOVE "OCTOPUS" FROM "FORMER". PUNCH OR CUT HOLE ⓡ WHERE FINGER OVERLAPS.

LEADER ⓢ GOES THROUGH HOLES AS INDICATED. HOOK HANGS IN GAP BETWEEN TENTACLES (SEE INSET BELOW).

OPTIONAL SPLIT SHOT ∗ ⓣ ATTACHED TO TENTACLES MAY IMPROVE ACTION.

EYES ⓤ MAY BE DRAWN ON OPPOSITE SIDE.

∗ OR SHEET LEAD

SUGGESTED HOOKUPS

TO ROD

12-14 GAUGE STAINLESS STEEL WIRE

6"

6"

10-15 lb TEST

ALTERNATE: 3-WAY SWIVEL

10-15 lb TEST LINE

20"

LEADER

#2 SPLIT RING

#3 SPLIT RING

DON'T TIE LEADER AT RING-SPLIT!

1 OR ⅞ HOOK

#2 SPLIT RING IS PULLED THRU HOLE ⓡ -- KEEPS HOOK IN POSITION, YET FREE TO MOVE.

The octopus is mounted on a paternoster rig—that is, a lead sinker to strike bottom and the lure hung higher up the line, clear of the ground. This can be done from a three-way swivel about twenty inches above the sinker, so the hooks are about a foot above the ground. This works fairly well, and I have caught many fish this way, but sometimes the lure tangles with the main line. This rig should be lowered while the boat is still moving so that the lure trails away from the main line.

This lure is very effective in hooking because when the fish bites, the body collapses and ensures a good hooking. When you extract the hook from the fish, the octopus can be slid up the line and out of the way.

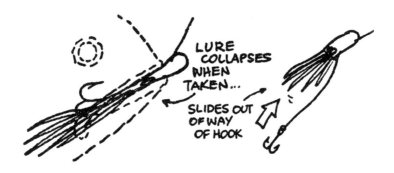

No doubt some trolling or casting lures rigged on a paternoster boom will get some fish, but except for the Buzz-Bomb, these lures are designed to deceive fish when they're moving horizontally. With vertical motion, a lure will resemble some living creature only occasionally in sight of a fish. The rubber octopus looks and acts like a live octopus whether it is stationary or moving up and down, so it gets more fish.

Weights

With this rig I use a 30-pound-test nylon reel line so that if the sinker snags, only it is lost, and the same with the lure.

A spherical or egg-shaped sinker is best, as these shapes give the most weight with the least surface area. They move easily through the water when keeping up with the drifting boat.

The tidal flow is faster at the surface than on the bottom, so there is always some slant to the line. Keep this to a minimum by avoiding fast water.

In depths of 60 feet or less, I use a four-ounce sinker, and in depths of 60 to 120 feet, a six-ounce. These weights were satisfactory in my fishing area, where the deepest reef was 120 feet down and tidal flow was rarely too strong.

You might need heavier sinkers in other areas, and more split shot clamped on to the hook link.

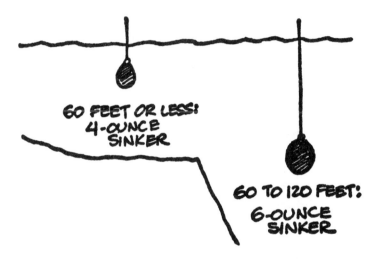

When the sinker reaches bottom, lower the line a few more inches to allow the boom to drop and allow time for the octopus to reach its tentacles-down position. Then give a few rod-tip movements—quick up and slow down—without lifting the sinker from the bottom.

This jerks the boom and gives action to the tentacles. Now raise the sinker a few inches above the bottom to let it catch up with the drifting boat before dropping again.

It is good to experiment in water about three feet deep, where you can see the action and learn the best way to manipulate the rod to get lifelike movements of the lure. These movements are those of a squid or octopus dropping to the bottom to get food with its outspread tentacles, then darting away with closed tentacles to escape the rockfish.

Avoiding Dogfish

Although dogfish are less of a bother with artificial lures, they are troublesome enough to make it worthwhile to use some wire in the hook link. The wire should connect to the boom with a short piece of nylon to save boom and sinker if the hook gets snagged or a large fish breaks away.

Be alert to every contour of the rocks below, reeling in or letting out as the depth changes, keeping the rod as near

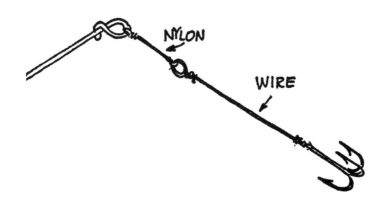

horizontal as possible so that if a fish bites it can be lifted immediately and held from holing in.

If the sinker gets snagged while you're drifting, row back well beyond the point where it caught and there is a good chance it can be pulled free.

Using the Tides

Because the fish bite either on a rising or falling tide, depending on the slope of the reef, it pays to choose the tidal movement that will drift you toward home while handling a large fish. Otherwise, you will have to row against the tide to get back to the reef and against the tide all the way home. If the drift takes you toward home while you're landing the last fish, there is that much less rowing to get there.

The logical procedure is to start out before the turn of the tide so you do not buck the current on the way to the fishing area. This will be at high or low slack depending on whether it is best for you to fish the falling or the rising tide.

Although the tide tables give the time of high and low water at spaced locations, it does not follow that the

current turns at those times or that there is a steadily increasing or decreasing current in between those times.

Often when the rise or fall is only a few feet, the water may be stationary for a while before, at, or after the forecast times. It may speed up or slow down during the rise or fall, and the fish may come on and go off feeding as the current moves, slows, and moves again.

Awareness of these facts added to some experience will help you get fish more often. Whenever you get a bite, note tidal conditions as well as location.

Other Tips

A boat designed for easy rowing is good for reef fishing. It is manoeuvrable and the rowing is excellent exercise, equal to a rowing machine but more pleasant and profitable. When fishing from a rowboat, tie the oars to the gunwale. If an oar gets knocked overboard when you are getting a fish up from the deeps, it could be difficult to regain it. One oar is not very effective, even in a light wind and tide.

It pays to make a fish box of a size and shape that suits the boat's bottom and can be pushed under the stern seat. This keeps the floor clear and less slippery. A large rockfish flopping around your ankles with spines erect diverts attention from the work in hand.

It is regrettable that practically all small boats these days are designed for outboard motors. They do not move freely with oars and drift badly in wind. Maybe when the air is sufficiently polluted, we will have good rowboats again.

Getting back to fish behaviour, weather conditions as well as tidal movements have some effect on the fish's feeding times. Izaac Walton observes in *The Compleat Angler* that trout do not bite so well during an easterly wind. I have found this to be true of rockfish as well.

But one never knows for sure. The year after I sold my dinghy, a new neighbour of mine who was interested in fishing asked if I would come along in her boat to help her get some driftfishing experience.

By the time we had launched the boat, an east wind had started. By the time we reached the reef, the wind was really too strong for fishing. We got on the marks, but with the wind and the tide the boat drifted too fast for a controlled drop of over 100 feet, the line taking too long a slant.

Returning to the marked spot, I decided to take a chance and let the reel run completely free the whole distance, despite the danger of a bad overrun. The sinker hit bottom and the overrun was not too bad. I reeled in the slack and there was a fish on. After netting it—a rockfish of about five pounds—we returned to marks and tried again, with exactly the same result. By this time, the sea was getting rough, so we came in.

Sometimes, when sufficient fish had been caught and there was still time to spare, I have searched for rocky outcrops using a rubber squid lure with no hooks.

It was remarkable and amusing how the fish would grab the lure and make repeated runs, pulling the line quite strongly, then letting go. The lure would then be immediately retaken, either by that fish or another.

One might think that fish would reject an artificial lure before the angler could strike the hook in, but apparently the rubber lure feels so much like a squid or octopus that the fish retains it in its mouth.

Repeatedly, when I dropped the lure and sinker 100 feet or more with some overrun, there was a fish already on when the line was recovered, showing that the fish did not at once reject the rubber lure as being something strange. Its reaction to a lead lure would likely be different.

It is possible to get a vertical drop when casting by using a specially designed sliding float. Experiments were conducted to design a sliding float that, after being cast a distance from the boat or shore, would drop and lift the lure vertically while moving slowly back. When reeled in fast, the lure would rise to the surface and come home.

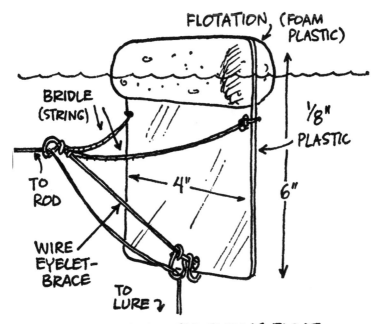

FLOTATION, (FOAM PLASTIC)

BRIDLE (STRING)

⅛" PLASTIC

TO ROD

4"

6"

WIRE EYELET-BRACE

TO LURE

SIDNEY GIRLING'S SLIDING FLOAT

CAST OFF SHORE, FLOAT'S LARGE, FLAT FACE RESISTS BEING PULLED THROUGH WATER. LINE IS FREE TO MOVE THROUGH EYELETS SO LURE CAN SINK TO DESIRED DEPTH, AND BE JIGGED, ETC.

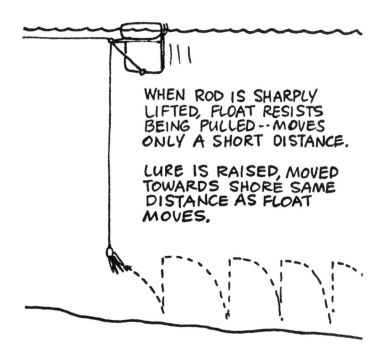

WHEN ROD IS SHARPLY
LIFTED, FLOAT RESISTS
BEING PULLED -- MOVES
ONLY A SHORT DISTANCE.

LURE IS RAISED, MOVED
TOWARDS SHORE SAME
DISTANCE AS FLOAT
MOVES.

Fishing is a gamble. One can never be quite sure of the outcome, but I hope this chapter will help others to better their luck.

Chapter 9
PERCH

When a school of these colourful mid-water swimmers is spotted cruising near a dock or moorage, there is always great excitement. Children in particular really love to catch these wily rascals.

PILE
SEAPERCH

The smaller shiner perch are usually easy to catch, but the larger striped perch and pile perch seem to ignore most baits dropped in front of their noses. This is especially true in bays and wharf areas where large numbers of pleasure boats congregate. The perch are just too wise. There are

HOHUM...

several techniques that seem to produce results. In order to catch perch, remember two things:

1. Find its natural food and prepare it so that it is easy to eat.
2. Present the bait in a natural manner.

Choosing a Bait

One of the best baits is our old friend the green pile worm, so effective for catching sole and flounder. (See Chapter 3 to find out how to get pile worms.) Break off small chunks of worm and completely cover the hook.

Tiny mussels, only a quarter- to a half-inch across, are excellent perch bait around docks and pilings, where they are a large part of the perch's natural food. Thread the mussel on the hook whole in the shell, breaking up the shell as little as possible.

Larger mussels can also be used, but they must be broken into pieces and are not as effective. Be sure to leave bits of shell clinging to the meat.

Shore crabs, the small crabs found by the thousands under rocks along the shore in the intertidal zone, are also good bait. Use small specimens and remove one or both claws. (Perch prefer a meal that doesn't fight back too hard!) Hook the crab through the side of the shell so that it can wiggle actively.

Ghost shrimp (also discussed in Chapter 3) can be deadly for perch. Use small ones whole, and break larger ones in half.

Clams, herring, and other baits are sometimes used, but they are often ineffective.

Presenting the Bait

Perch are very fussy eaters, so the bait must be presented carefully and naturally:

1. **Use light line and small hooks**. A No. 4 or 5 hook is about right. You can use line as light as four- for five-pound-test, but I find ten-pound to be light enough for most places. You might use ten-pound line with six-pound leader, tied with a tiny, tiny swivel about four to six feet from the hook.

2. **Do not use a sinker**. Letting the bait fall naturally through the water seems to be one of the most important factors in catching perch. A bait being dragged down by even a small split shot weight is enough to scare off most perch. Let the bait fall freely to the bottom or through the fish school,

then retrieve it and repeat the free-fall process. No cast is necessary when dock fishing. Just drop the line in the water and keep it slack for free falling.

If you can't make the line sink without a weight (due to current), try tossing it upcurrent so it will drift down toward you, sinking as it comes. As a last resort, put a tiny weight right next to the swivel about four feet from the bait.

3. **Be inconspicuous**. Perch can see you as well or better than you can see them. Don't make sudden moves or wave your arms to point out the school to your friends. Talking or even shouting won't disturb the fish, as sound waves don't carry well into water. Any stamping, banging, or vibration on the dock (or boat), however, will be carried instantly into the water and may scare the fish.

4. **Look for the fish**. If you lie down on the dock with your face near the water, and in the shade, you will usually be able to see the school of perch. Anticipate its direction and drop your bait to flutter down a few feet in front of it. If your bait is right, several perch should rush up to inspect it, and one will suck it into its mouth!

5. **Try different times of day**. Like all fish, perch feed more actively at certain times. Early morning and evening are often good times. In busy marinas, try the times when not many boats are moving and things are peaceful and quiet.

Chapter 10

SURF PERCH

These sporty fighters are quite similar to their quiet-water cousins, but they live in a much more active environment. They are found in the active surf off rocky or sandy shorelines along the open coast. They are not shy, fussy eaters like their relatives—they will grab aggressively at baits presented to them.

Casting or spinning outfits are best for this type of fishing. Use a rig with a sinker at the extreme end.

Clams, mussels, and pile worms are good bait. Anglers also report excellent catches using Dungeness crab legs for bait.

Chapter 11

GREENLING
(KELP COD OR KELP TROUT)

These sporty fish are most often found around kelp beds and rocky shorelines. They have small mouths, so smaller hooks (No. 2 to 4) are often effective with bait. Greenling will also strike small artificial lures. A wet fly cast with a spinning outfit and retrieved slowly near the bottom can produce good results. The greenling is not an important fish to either the sport or commercial fisherman.

ROCK GREENLING

Chapter 12

JIGGING WITH ARTIFICIAL LURES

Jigging is increasingly popular for salmon fishing, with newer and more sophisticated lures moving in to compete with the traditional Buzz-Bombs, Stingsildas, Pirkens, and others. These jigs have always been effective for bottomfish as well and, using techniques discovered in experiments with our underwater camera, can be even more so.

Jigging with artificial lures imitates the action of severely wounded or stunned baitfish, which just flutter down toward the bottom. A shorter, somewhat stiffer rod is best, and there are many different jigging strokes used.

I had the opportunity to talk and fish with the late Rex Field, pioneer developer of the Buzz-Bomb. He told me that most people jerk his lures far too hard. "Fish can't catch a jig that's moving too fast," Rex said. Our underwater camera proved him correct.

We found that salmon and bottomfish would make one or two passes at the lure, then give up quickly if they didn't catch it. To our surprise, even short pulls were difficult to catch, and we set out to design jigs that would flutter down more slowly and be easier to catch.

We tried lures of lighter metal and lures with plastic "wings," but they were too hard to control and get an effective action. Then we added a forked spinner, similar to the one used on our trolling lure. It worked well. The spinner acted like a parachute and slowed the lure just enough that the fish caught it much more easily. As a bonus, the flash of the spinner and the sonic vibration focussed the strike at the tail of the lure where our sticky-sharp hooks were waiting. This lure, called The Lure by Charlie White—Jigging Model, is no longer available in sporting-goods stores, but you can order a sample pack of five jigs from Saltaire Publishing for $25 plus $6 shipping and handling. (Sorry, no credit cards; cheque only.) Send to 11046 Chalet Rd., Sidney, BC, V8L 5M2.

Jigging for bottomfish is quite simple. Drop the lure until it hits the bottom, then jig up and down with short strokes— no more than twelve to eighteen inches. To be most effective, the lure should bump the bottom on almost every stroke. When jigging on rocky bottoms, the lures will get scarred up very quickly, but they still catch fish.

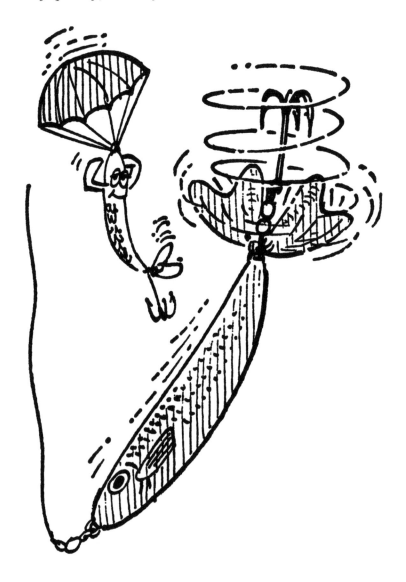

As I mentioned earlier, the productivity of jigging lures more than doubled when we added a small chunk of bait to the hooks. This was especially true with sole, flounder, and other flatfish. A couple of short jigs followed by leaving the baited lure motionless on the bottom was usually a deadly technique.

Jigging lures are often more effective when bent into a banana shape. This bend allows a slower, wobbly flutter, which our camera showed stimulated strike activity.

Chapter 13

HOW TO CLEAN AND FILLET BOTTOMFISH

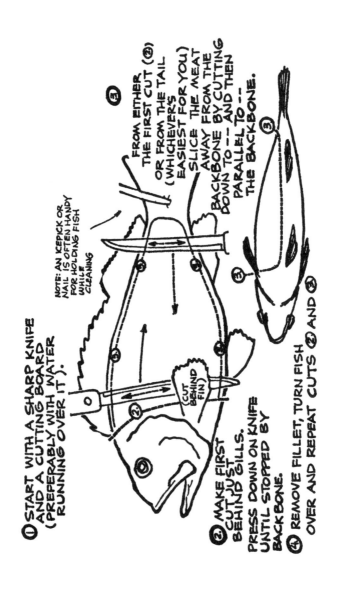

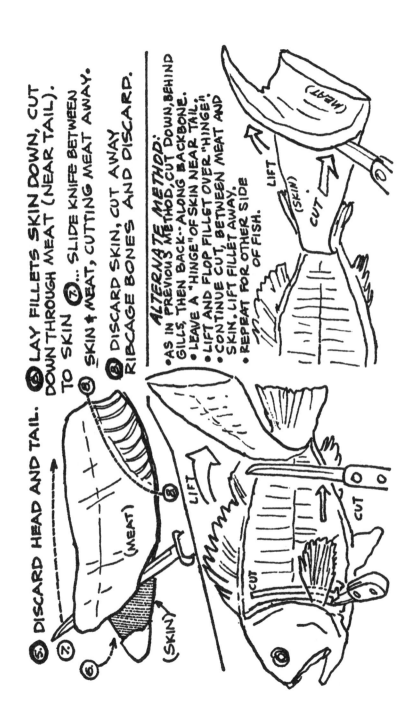

5. DISCARD HEAD AND TAIL.

6. LAY FILLETS SKIN DOWN, CUT DOWN THROUGH MEAT (NEAR TAIL) TO SKIN.

7. ...SLIDE KNIFE BETWEEN SKIN & MEAT, CUTTING MEAT AWAY.

8. DISCARD SKIN, CUT AWAY RIBCAGE BONES AND DISCARD.

ALTERNATE METHOD:
- AS IN PREVIOUS METHOD, CUT DOWN, BEHIND GILLS, THEN BACK— ALONG BACKBONE.
- LEAVE A "HINGE" OF SKIN NEAR TAIL.
- LIFT AND FLOP FILLET OVER "HINGE".
- CONTINUE CUT, BETWEEN MEAT AND SKIN. LIFT FILLET AWAY.
- REPEAT FOR OTHER SIDE OF FISH.

(MEAT) (SKIN) LIFT CUT

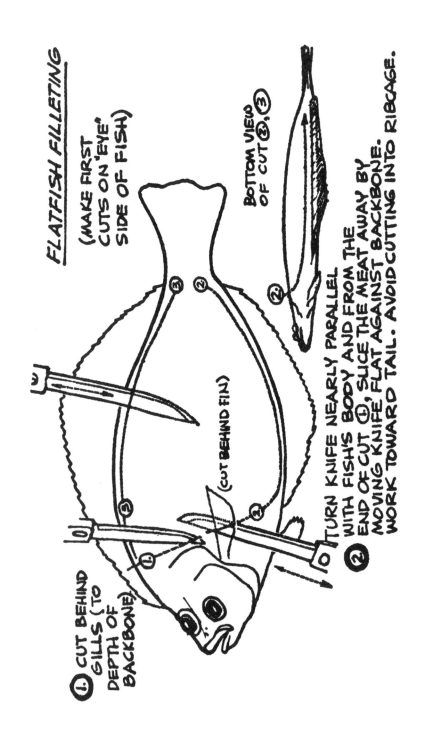

FLATFISH FILLETING

(MAKE FIRST CUTS ON "EYE" SIDE OF FISH)

BOTTOM VIEW OF CUT ②, ③

1. CUT BEHIND GILLS (TO DEPTH OF BACKBONE).

(CUT BEHIND FIN)

2. TURN KNIFE NEARLY PARALLEL WITH FISH'S BODY AND FROM THE END OF CUT ①, SLICE THE MEAT AWAY BY MOVING KNIFE FLAT AGAINST BACKBONE. WORK TOWARD TAIL. AVOID CUTTING INTO RIBCAGE.

③ REPEAT PREVIOUS CUT, BUT FROM TOP OF FISH'S BACK, STARTING AT BEGINNING OF CUT ①.

④ PEEL MEAT & SKIN AWAY FROM FISH -- STILL ATTACHED NEAR THE TAIL -- AND LAY IT OUT FLAT.

⑤ CUT MEAT AWAY FROM THE SKIN. PEEL MEAT AWAY AS YOU MAKE CUT -- THEN CLEAN ANY FIN, INTESTINE, RIB BONES FROM THE MEAT.

⑥ TURN FISH OVER, REPEAT ① THRU ⑤. IF YOU WISH, THE "BOTTOM" SKIN CAN BE LEFT ON THE MEAT, AS IT'S USUALLY QUITE TENDER.

⑦ DISCARD HEAD & BONES; COOK OR FREEZE MEAT TO SUIT.

(*LARGER FISH -- SUCH AS HALIBUT -- ARE USUALLY GUTTED AND CUT CROSSWAYS INTO STEAKS OR CHUNKS.)

FISHING DIARY

Date	Time	Lure and Colour	Depth	Weather & Tide

Species	Weight	Where

FISHING REGULATIONS

Do not go fishing or crabbing along the west coast without checking current government regulations.

The *B.C. Tidal Waters Sport Fishing Guide*, published annually by Fisheries and Oceans Canada, is available free of charge at sporting-goods stores, marinas, and similar outlets. The guide contains all current regulations governing sport fishing for salmon, halibut, rockfish, crabs, oysters, and other species.

Current sport-fishing regulations are also available by visiting the following websites.

B.C. Ministry of Water, Land and Air: Fresh Water Regulations Protection
http://www.bcfisheries.gov.bc.ca/rec/fresh/regulations/synopsis.html

Fisheries and Oceans Canada: Salt Water Regulations
http://www-comm.pac.dfo-mpo.gc.ca/pages/sfg/default_e.htm

Alaska Department of Fish and Game
http://www.sf.adfg.state.ak.us/statewide/html/reghome.stm

Washington Department of Fish and Wildlife
http://www.wa.gov/wdfw/fish/regs/fishregs.htm

Oregon Department of Fish and Wildlife
http://www.dfw.state.or.us/

California Fish and Game Commission
http://www.dfg.ca.gov/fg_comm/fishregs.html

Cover Photos: Robert H. Jones
Front cover—Choon Fong with a yelloweye rockfish and Derrick Stevenson with a chicken halibut (Codfather Charters, Port Hardy). Back cover—Top row, left to right: Vera Jones and a 22-pound yelloweye rockfish (Silver Fox Charters, Port Hardy); Ralph Shaw and Ken Jenkins with an 85-pound halibut (Codfather Charters); Ray Uhl with a 45-pound lingcod (Silver Fox Charters). Centre: Billy Finlay and a brown rockfish. Bottom: Ralph Shaw and Ian Andersen with a yelloweye rockfish (Silver Fox Charters).